How to Write
a Marketing Plan
for Health Care
Organizations

About the Author

William J. Winston is the Dean of the School of Health Services Management at Golden Gate University in San Francisco, California. Mr. Winston's instructional areas are in graduate-level Economic Analysis for Health Organizations and Marketing Planning and Strategy Development for Health Organizations. In addition, he has been actively involved in developing and lecturing in marketing seminars and workshops for health professionals for most of the last decade. In fact, the graduate course taught by Mr. Winston in Health Marketing was one of the first ever offered in the country for practitioners. Many marketing and economic papers and speeches are given for health and medical organizations each year.

Mr. Winston is also the Senior Marketing Editor of three national journals, *Health Marketing Quarterly, The Journal of Professional Services Marketing,* and *Psychotherapy Practice Marketing and Development Reports* for The Haworth Press, Inc., New York, New York. Books edited by Mr. Winston include *Marketing for the Group Practice, Marketing for Mental Health Services, Marketing Long-Term and Senior Care Services, Innovations in Hospital Marketing, Marketing Ambulatory Care Services, Marketing Strategies for Human and Social Services,* and *Handbook on Advertising for Health Care Organizations.* Additional articles are published in the areas of economic analysis and applied health marketing.

William Winston is a Managing Associate of an Albany, California-based services marketing consulting firm, Professional Services Marketing Group. Through the years the author has developed hundreds of marketing plans for all types of health and human services in his capacity as an educator and consultant.

Formerly, Mr. Winston was President of Winston & Associates, an economic analysis consulting firm and Principal of Business Economics Development Institute. His graduate education in health administration and planning was completed at the Johns Hopkins University in Baltimore, Maryland and his doctoral dissertation is being completed in business administration with Nova University in Florida.

Mr. Winston is on the Board of Directors of the American College of Health Care Marketing. He is also very active in the International Health Economics and Management Institute, Health Care Division of the Academy of Management, Association of Western Hospitals, American Management Association, American Health Planning Association, American Medical Writers Association, American Health Consultants, and other major national health and management associations.

How to Write a Marketing Plan for Health Care Organizations

William J. Winston

Golden Gate University
Professional Services Marketing Group

The Haworth Press
New York • London

How to Write a Marketing Plan for Health Care Organizations is a monographic supplement to the journal *Health Marketing Quarterly,* Volume 2, 1985. It is not supplied as part of the subscription to the journal, but is available from the publisher at an additional charge.

Reprint-2007

The Haworth Press, Inc., 10 Alice Street, Binghamton, NY 13904–1580
EUROSPAN/Haworth, 3 Henrietta Street, London WC2E 8LU England

Library of Congress Cataloging in Publication Data
Winston, William J.
    How to write a marketing plan for health care organizations.

    "A monographic supplement to the journal Health marketing quarterly, vol. 2, 1985"—T.p. verso.
    Bibliography: p.
    1. Medical care—Marketing. 2. Health planning. 3. Health facilities—
Administration. I. Health marketing quarterly. v. 2 (Supplement) II. Title.
[DNLM: 1. Marketing of Health Services—organization & administration. W1 HE414D
v.2 Suppl. / W 74 W783h]
RA410.5.W557   1985   362.1'1'0688   85-10037
ISBN 0-86656-450-0

CONTENTS

Preface

The environment of health care organizations is ever-changing. The development of effective strategies to take advantage of opportunities presented by this environment requires a dynamic process. Unfortunately, health care organizations have traditionally taken a defensive position in reaction to environmental changes. The 1980s have brought tremendous changes in government spending for health care, regulations, reimbursement, and in the private/public mix of delivering health services. This new environment demands today's administrator, marketer, and planner to be constantly monitoring this environment for the identification of potential opportunities to pursue and risks to avoid.

Marketplace analysis has become the most important component of managing health care organizations. It is imperative for health care executives to plan for the future based on this market analysis. In other words, total strategic planning for a health organization should focus on the marketplace with consumers and providers in mind. The marketing aspect of planning should be the keystone component in the organization's total strategic plan. Marketing planning allows for health managers to be better able to predict, adapt, and take advantage of environmental changes. Strategic planning and market orientation need to be integrated in all health organizations. Strategic planning and marketing provide strong complementary approaches for survival and potential growth.

Health care marketing has become "the name of the game" for the 1980s. Marketing is the buzzword of the 1980s throughout the economy. Marketers are becoming as important in the 1980s as financial and operational people were in health care during the 1970s. Once it was enough for health care organizations to provide a basic service and assume it would market itself. Today the organizations are asking what services they should be providing and to whom they should be marketing them. Mass marketing in health care is a thing of the past. Service differentiation and sophisticated market targeting are becoming the key ingredients. To remain competitive you have to behave like a shark in the water. Anytime you stop swimming you are going to drown and your health care competitors will take over your niche in the marketplace. Health care organizations need not just to "market," but must become sophisticated in marketing. One aspect of building a base for sophistication is to make use of the tool of strategic marketing planning.

This short book is based on my experiences as a health economist and marketer in education and as a health marketing consultant. The methodology has been successfully implemented in hundreds of marketing plans for a wide array of different health organizations. From my experiences I have identified most failures in marketing related to not developing a plan of action. Typically the organization has desired results without being willing to allocate the time and money to lay out a thorough planning process. Unfortunately most health marketing programs move ahead to strategy implementation before a solid foundation is formed. Strategic marketing planning does not assure performance, but it provides a disciplined approach to marketing the health facility and can minimize failures. There is an old saying that a marketer needs to "plan the work and work the plan." This means that all the planning in the world by itself is useless. Careful implementation of the plan must be the final step in the process.

The strategic marketing plan specifies who will do what, where, when, and how to accomplish the organizational goals established by the health organization. The basic steps to the marketing planning process are described in sequence of the chapters presented. Of course, the sequencing can be variable depending upon the interests and talents of the marketer. The major steps described for development are:

— Marketing missions
— Marketing goals and objectives
— Audit and environmental analysis
— Segmentation and targeting
— Market positioning
— Strategies and tactics
— Control system
— Budget and time line
— Administration of the marketing function

The reader should be able to use this methodology as a strong framework for marketing their hospitals, HMOs, PPOs, ambulatory care centers, group practices, long-term care institutions, clinics, and other types of health facilities and programs. The methodology has been written, edited, and presented in a pragmatic manner with multiple applications. The final chapter of the text provides an actual sample marketing plan for reference. Three appendices have been added for basic information on advertising, using consultants, working with the media, and integrating computers into the marketing process.

The need for marketing planning has never been greater, as are the market opportunities for health professionals during the 1980s. It is hoped that this book will be a valuable resource to assist in maximizing the cost-benefit of your health organization's investment in marketing.

The first chapter provides a basic framework for better understanding the applicability of marketing to health services and surveys the key marketing terminology used throughout the text. The second chapter provides a thorough description of the strategic marketing planning process and the main reasons for developing a marketing plan for the health facility. The focus of the book is oriented toward being able to market to a variety of groups such as the general public, medical providers, staff, legislators, regulatory agencies, and other health organizations in the community. The major strength of the book is achieved through the emphasis on marketing tools based on a firm theoretical base. Therefore, the text can be used by health practitioners and students alike. All of the material has been tested extensively in the classroom and in the "so-called" real world. This text can be used effectively as a primary or secondary text in health marketing, health planning, or non-profit marketing college courses.

ACKNOWLEDGMENTS

Special thanks are due to the hundreds of graduate students, consulting clients, practitioner faculty, and professional associates who have assisted me in testing these concepts and methodology. The graduate students within the School of Health Services Management at Golden Gate University have worked hard in preparing marketing plans for health organizations in the San Francisco Bay Area as part of my course requirements. In addition, thanks must go to the many different marketing professionals around the country who have been willing to share their expertise with me. Of course no major project is achieved without tremendous personal support. My love and gratitude are extended to my wife, Ms. Rosanna Pribilovics, for her moral support through the years. Last, but not least, I want to thank Al Zahn, Dean Emeritus at Golden Gate University, for his trust and confidence in my abilities and ambitions. To all of these people I am deeply grateful for their support and guidance.

Chapter 1

Basic Health Care Marketing Principles

INTRODUCTION

Health care marketing has become an important management tool for health administrators during recent years. It has only been an accepted scope of study in research during the last decade. However, marketing has been used in health care for centuries. This is documented in the cases of public health campaigns during the 17th and 18th centuries. It has also been extensively utilized by pharmaceutical firms, hospital supply firms, health maintenance organizations, and public health agencies during the last forty years.

The recognition and acceptance of marketing in health care during the 1980s is similar to the rise in importance of finance during the 1970s. Finance was considered the "savior" during this decade as budgeting and financial forecasting became popular in health organizations. Budget directors and controllers were promoted to vice-presidency positions. In comparison, marketing has become the name of the game for the 1980s. Directors of public relations are being promoted to vice-presidents of marketing and planning. Unfortunately, marketing is perceived by many administrators and providers as the future savior. As it will be discussed later, no management tool by itself is a savior.

The development of health care marketing is entering its second phase. During the first half of the 1980s, most of the attention was placed on answering the key questions "what is marketing?" and "why do we need to market?" The second phase during the middle and second half of the 1980s is addressing tools, applications, and sophisticated methodologies for practical use by health administrators and providers. This text describes one of the most important marketing tools: writing a formal marketing plan for the health organization/facility. It is applicable for health managers in all health delivery systems. Before outlining the steps to the marketing planning process in detail, the basic principles of health marketing are surveyed.

WHAT IS HEALTH CARE MARKETING?

HEALTH MARKETING is an organized discipline for understanding: 1) how a health marketplace works; 2) the role in which the health organization can render optimum services to the marketplace; 3) mechanisms for adjusting production capabilities for meeting consumer demand; and 4) how the organization can assure patient satisfaction.

COMPONENTS OF HEALTH CARE MARKETING

Marketing includes a variety of functions, such as:

1. MARKETING RESEARCH which describes the collection of information about an organization's internal and external environment;
2. MARKETING PLANNING which is the framework for identifying, collecting, and capturing select segments in the marketplace;
3. MARKETING STRATEGY DEVELOPMENT which relates to new service development and actions to be taken for taking advantage of opportunities and gaps in the marketplace;
4. PUBLIC RELATIONS that describes the action of communicating with the publics that interact with the health organization;
5. FUND DEVELOPMENT which is the solicitation of resources for the organization or special services;
6. COMMUNITY RELATIONS which act as a liaison with the publics served;
7. PATIENT LIAISON who acts as intermediator between the provision of care and the patient;
8. RECRUITMENT for medical providers or staff;
9. INTERNAL MARKETING which includes staff development in marketing, marketing role expectation, and triage efficiency; and
10. CONTRACTING for new modes of delivery, such as preferred provider organizations, IPAs, or HMOs.

MARKETING AS A SUBSYSTEM OF MANAGEMENT

Marketing is one function of management. It is integrated with other management subsystems of PRODUCTION, FINANCE, and HUMAN RESOURCES. MARKETING determines the needs of the consumer in the marketplace and lays out a plan for satisfying these needs. Production, finance, and human resources follow this lead and initiate the process of satisfying consumer needs through service provision.

TYPES OF HEALTH MARKETING

There are many applications of marketing in health care. Some of these applications include marketing for: services, patients, new staff, donors, social causes, creative ideas, goodwill, staff morale, public relations, provider relations, community relations, political and lobbyist activities, new products, fund raising, patient relations, and contracting.

BASIC PREMISES OF HEALTH CARE MARKETING

Before implementing a marketing program, some basic premises must be established about marketing. These include:

1. The patient is a client. There is an exchange process occurring between the consumer and supplier. Even with extensive insurance coverage, every client exchanges time, money, discomfort, and anxiety in obtaining a health service.

2. The best outcome of marketing is a patient or client referral.

3. All providers must continue to assess the effectiveness of their services and not be satisfied to assume they are good just because people use them.

4. Like a new suit of clothes, services must pass initial examination by clients and continue to hold up after the time of initial purchase by the consumer.

5. Marketing is a management tool. It does not offer all the answers to effectively operating a successful organization. It must be blended among financial management, human resource management, strategic planning, and economic analysis.

TEN KEY QUESTIONS ANSWERED BY MARKETING

Marketing supplies answers to the following basic questions:

1. What business are we in and what is the purpose for the organization's existence?
2. Who is our client?
3. What does our client need?
4. Which markets should the organization be addressing?
5. What are the strengths of the organization?
6. What are the weaknesses of the organization that need to be attended to?
7. Who are our competitors?
8. Which groups (segments/targets) do we want to serve in the community?
9. What are our marketing strategies to communicate to these groups?
10. What strategies should we develop related to pricing, promotion, access, and the types of services offered?

TRADITIONAL VERSUS NEWER MARKETING CONCEPTS

The traditional method for understanding marketing is demonstrated by the following relationship:

PRODUCT + SELLING AND PROMOTION =
PROFITS THROUGH SALES VOLUME

This relationship is based on the traditional "Madison Avenue" aspect of selling being the most important part of marketing. Selling is only one function of marketing and the real outcome of marketing will be client satisfaction. This is exemplified in the following relationship:

UNDERSTANDING CLIENT NEEDS + INTEGRATED
MARKETING = PROFITS THROUGH CLIENT
SATISFACTION

Integrated marketing includes RESEARCHING THE ENVIRONMENT, DEVELOPING A MARKETING PLAN, and CRE-

ATING COMMUNICATION STRATEGIES BASED ON THE RESEARCH AND PLANNING.

Marketing programs which have failed are partly due to a lack of preliminary research, analysis, and planning before implementing communication strategies.

The SELLING CONCEPT focuses on the services, is solely dependent on public relations, and increases revenues through volume. The MARKETING CONCEPT focuses on consumer needs, uses integrated marketing, and increases revenues through consumer satisfaction.

The marketing concept refers to the study or practice of marketing strategies designed to assess consumer preferences about existing or proposed services, implies a direction to deliver services which meet these preferences and needs, and establishes a criterion of effectiveness so that consumers' health needs are satisfied by the services.

PUBLICS, MARKET, EXCHANGE PROCESS

Every organization conducts its business in an environment of both internal and external PUBLICS. A public is a distinct group of people or organizations that have an actual or potential interest or impact on the health organization. For example, publics for a hospital would be the media, government agencies, other health organizations, the population in the community, medical providers, and its employees.

A health organization functions through the exchange process in a MARKET. A market is a process where a minimum of two groups possess resources they want to exchange for some benefit. It is the matching of demand and supply.

Every marketplace has an EXCHANGE. Exchange involves mutual satisfaction of the groups involved. There must be two parties and each must have something that is valued by the other party. For example, patients exchange time, money, discomfort, anxiety, and inconvenience for the services provided.

THE MARKETING MIX

Just as everyone who has studied economics remembers the basic principles of demand and supply, a marketer always is able to fall back on the foundation of the MARKETING MIX. The marketing mix is the mixture or blending of select characteristics of the organization that are utilized to achieve some marketing objective and communicate with a select public.

There are four components of the marketing mix:

1. *PRICING:* This is becoming an important area of health marketing. It can include the direct cost, indirect costs, opportunity costs, discounting, prepayment plans, contracting, co-payments, credit terms, and deductibles. All organizations must price their services to be able to earn a normal profit which is the amount necessary to keep operations and some capital investment going. Normal profits are a regular part of operating costs. Some factors which must be included in the pricing of a service include: demand characteristics for the service, pricing by competitors, consumer expectations for pricing, possible effects on other services provided by the organization, legal aspects, competitive reaction to changes in prices, profitability, and the psychology of the consumer. Some pricing strategies include COMPETITIVE PRICING which sets the price at the "going rate" in the marketplace; MARKET PENETRATION which sets a below-competition price to capture additional market share; SKIMMING which is useful in launching a new service for which the initial price might sustain a high price; and VARIABLE PRICING based on seasonal fluctuations.

2. *PRODUCT:* Marketing strategies can be developed related to the physical characteristics of the products and services provided. These characteristics include: quality of care, atmospherics, style, size, brand name, service, warranties, types of medical providers, quality of staff interactions, level of technology, and research activities. A health organization must have an attractive service which offers some value to the consumer. These values have to satisfy the needs of the consumer. Every new service needs to be researched, have the market screened for potential acceptance, tested for performance levels, and finally, launched into the market selectively. Typically, health organizations offer an array of different services. Therefore, a PRODUCT PORTFOLIO needs to be established which plans out the kind of PRODUCT/SERVICE MIX most readily acceptable for the market served.

3. *PLACE:* A key aspect of developing marketing strategies is related to access to the service. The place component of the marketing mix consists of the characteristics of service distribution, modes of delivery, location, transportation, availability, hours and days opened, appointments, parking, waiting time, and other access con-

siderations. Some strategies have included opening a health center on weekends or in the evenings, hiring security guards for evenings, lighting parking lots, possessing excellent triage systems for small amounts of waiting time, locating near public transportation, and changing the mode of delivery to include home services.

4. *PROMOTION:* The promotional strategies relate to methods for communicating to the publics. Promotion can include advertising, public relations, personal selling, sales promotion, and publicity. A PROMOTIONAL MIX needs to be established by blending advertising, sales promotion, personal selling, health education, and publicity. The three main ingredients of external communication are the provision of INFORMATION about the service, PERSUASION, and INFLUENCE to use the service if needed. When using promotional strategies, the basic factors to consider are: the availability of funds, the stage of the life cycle the service is in (see next section), the nature of the service, the nature of the market, and the intensity of the competition.

SERVICE/PRODUCT LIFE CYCLE

Just as the human life cycle, every product or service experiences its own unique life cycle. This life cycle includes phases of INTRODUCTION, GROWTH, MATURITY, and DECLINE.

Introduction Phase: In this phase the service is planned for, researched, and developed. It is then introduced into the marketplace for the first time. During this phase, it is usual to experience a considerable amount of technical innovation, research and development, experimentation, initial production and delivery problems, the determination of modes of delivery and channels for distribution, and the development and emergence of the initial marketing mix and promotional strategies. Most strategies relate to informing the publics about the service, educating them about their cost-effectiveness, and instructing them on how to use and obtain the service.

Growth Phase: Expansion occurs and the service becomes accepted by the community. Increased utilization materializes and more resources are inputed into the production process. Typically, new channels for distribution and delivery are created, competitors start to enter the marketplace, attempts are made to entrench the new service in the market by brand loyalty, and emphasis is placed on developing a strong referral network by concentrating on consumer satisfaction.

Maturity Phase: Most health organizations are in the maturity phase. This is usually the longest phase for the organization. The market becomes oversaturated with many similar services and competitors. Utilization and revenues tend to level off. Innovation is attempted by modifying the original service to attract new publics or segments, the development of new services begins, and promotion tends to emphasize the reputation of the organization, its history, quality of service, and reliability and integrity.

Decline: All organizations will not experience a major decline phase which ends in the termination of the organization or service. Utilization and revenues usually decline in this phase dramatically, competition becomes aggressive, many new services are attempted for salvation of the organization, and planned obsolescence is a possibility for the original service. Of course, many products and services have indeterminate life cycles while others are very transitory due to trends. No sooner is one service started than another must be in the design stage to eventually replace or complement it.

THE MARKETING PLANNING PROCESS

A key tool in marketing is the development of a formal written MARKETING PLAN. Unfortunately, most health organizations jump the gun and concentrate on implementing strategies and tactics before a solid foundation is established through planning. Many marketing failures occur due to the omission of the planning process. A marketing plan is a framework which lays out the specific steps to market the health service. Marketing planning allows the organizations to: evaluate the marketplace, identify strengths and weaknesses, identify segments to market to, penetrate the market, capture a select market share, and achieve a key positioning/image within the community.

There are four main components of marketing: ORGANIZATION, RESEARCH, CREATIVITY PHASE, and CONTROL.

The ORGANIZATIONAL PHASE of the marketing planning process begins by setting up a marketing committee within the organization. This committee should minimally include the director of marketing, executive director, director of patient services, and a representative from the board. It is important to obtain organizational support for the function of marketing. The committee can be helpful in developing relationships and support from providers, board members, and the staff. A marketing philosophy has to be established by the organization for effectiveness. The MARKETING MISSION should be established. It will answer "What business are we in?", "What is the purpose for our existence?", and "Why are we marketing and what main markets are we addressing?" The mission lays a framework for developing the entire marketing program. Then MARKETING GOALS AND OBJECTIVES give us some guidelines for developing the specifics of the program. Marketing goals will outline broad desired results or outcomes we hope to achieve through marketing. The objectives will define the goals by describing specific, measurable outcomes that are to be achieved. For example, a goal could be a broad statement related to increasing utilization. The objective would specify a certain percentage of increased utilization within a time constraint.

The second phase of marketing is the MARKETING RESEARCH OR AUDITING area. Marketing research provides key internal and external information as background to identify trends in the marketplace and help in creating cost-effective strategies. The audit should include the collection of information related to: DEMOGRAPHIC FACTORS (i.e., age, sexual mix of the population, region, county size, population growth, climate, etc.); ECONOMIC FACTORS (i.e., income, occupations, industry trends, etc.); PSYCHOGRAPHIC FACTORS (i.e., lifestyle, values, interests, personality traits, etc.); INDUSTRIAL FACTORS (i.e, competition, health system trends, legislation, lobbyist activities, new modes of delivery, reimbursement trends, etc.); and INTERNAL FACTORS (i.e., quantity and quality of staff, training needs, staff knowledge of marketing and their role in marketing the organization, etc.). After the collection of background information is completed, an OPPORTUNITY/RISK ANALYSIS is done. This activity identifies trends from the audit that possibly relate to potential new services and gaps in the marketplace that our organization could fill. The analysis also examines risks to avoid. The outcome of this phase is the identification of market TARGETS that will be marketed to by our programs. First the audit should allow the administrator to subdivide the marketplace into distinct segments which might merit an individualized marketing program. After the development of this laundry list of segments, a more finite list of primary and secondary targets can be made. It is not feasible to market to every segment. Therefore, the marketing strategies are directed toward select market targets in the marketplace. The primary and secondary targets will consist of those publics in the market which the organization can serve effectively and offer the greatest opportunities.

The three main types of segmentation and targeting are UNDIF-FERENTIATED, DIFFERENTIATED, and CONCENTRATED. Undifferentiated targeting relates to mass marketing whereby it is hoped that the right targets will be communicated to by marketing to everyone. Since finances are limited throughout health care it is important to differentiate your marketing activities. Differentiated targeting identifies a few key targets to address. Concentrated targeting limits the targets to one or two select groups. It has been proven to be cost-effective to approach targeting from a differentiated or concentrated approach rather than from an undifferentiated approach.

The CREATIVE PHASE of the planning process includes the development of STRATEGIES AND TACTICS. Strategies and tactics are the specific actions which will be taken to communicate to select target groups with the satisfaction of specific goals and objectives in mind. The first step for strategy development is to develop POSITIONING STRATEGIES. Positioning provides an understanding of how people perceive the organization and identifies how the organization is unique in the marketplace. The underlying philosophy of marketing is to position the organization in the minds of the consumers. Positioning can be related to the quality of the staff, the location, pricing of services, access, and other characteristics of the organization that are unique. The marketing strategies and tactics can be developed by itemizing actions that are directed at marketing a select service. An example of a strategy would be the decision to advertise to a select target group. The tactic would then describe the type of ad, location, size, and color. Strategies can be developed according to the four Ps of the marketing mix discussed earlier: PRICE, PLACE, PRODUCT, and PROMOTION. They can also be developed according to the phase of the life cycle in which the organization fits.

The CONTROL PHASE of the marketing process includes developing a MARKETING BUDGET, IMPLEMENTATION TIME LINE, ORGANIZATIONAL CHART FOR MARKETING, and a CONTROL SYSTEM to monitor the plan's effectiveness. The budget forecasts all of the direct and indirect expenses for developing, implementing, and controlling the marketing plan. The time line outlines specific dates and times for the planning, strategy implementation, and control phases. The organizational chart describes the lines of authority and reporting requirements for the marketing function. The directors of marketing should definitely have planning, public relations, and fund development reporting to them. Direct access to the executive director and a representative of the board may prevent future implementation problems. The control system outlines when and how the marketing program will be monitored for effectiveness. The control system measures the performance of the marketing program against the expected outcomes, or in this case, the goals and objectives that were established in the first phase of the marketing plan. It provides a guideline for pinpointing any problems or deviations and a mechanism for adjusting the plan if necessary, and it accumulates data for future marketing planning.

Marketing plans are essential for successful marketing programs. However, planning does not assure success but it does provide a disciplined approach to marketing and can minimize risks. The marketing plan specifies by service who will do what, when, where, and how, to accomplish the marketing goals and objectives in the most efficient manner. The plan identifies opportunities, coordinates efforts to attract new clients, stimulates creativity in the organization, supports innovation, and allocates resources more effectively. There is an old saying that a marketer needs to "plan the work and work the plan." This means that a lot of planning is useless unless it is implemented carefully. Implementation is as important as developing a plan. The plan is a guideline. It can be changed and adjusted over a long time frame. This is important because marketing is also a long-term process. Results do not occur overnight. Unrealistic expectations about marketing being a miracle worker are one of the major causes of failure. Marketing can be a major management resource for the health organization if it is understood and applied effectively through the planning process.

SUMMARY FOR CHAPTER 1:
BASIC PRINCIPLES OF HEALTH CARE MARKETING

The role of marketing in health care organizations has never been more important. This is reflective of the most competitive health care marketplace in history. Health organizations are examining new and entrepreneural ways in which to deliver their services in response to this changing marketplace. Despite the fact that marketing has been used for centuries in health care, most health care administrators have not been trained in marketing techniques. This first chapter provides a brief summary, and for some an introduction, of the basic theoretical concepts in marketing. Many of these concepts will be discussed in greater detail and with applications during later chapters.

This first chapter should provide a foundation of 1) what marketing is; 2) its applications; 3) major theoretical concepts utilized in the scope of study; and 4) a brief introduction to the role of the marketing planning function. The next chapter elaborates on the strategic marketing planning process as a continuation of foundation material for the actual steps to use in developing a marketing plan.

Chapter 2

Introduction to Marketing Planning

WHAT IS A MARKETING PLAN?

A MARKETING PLAN is a framework which lays out the specific steps for marketing the health organization. Marketing plans have become indispensable in health facilities that want to successfully compete in today's marketplace. Before being able to commit marketing resources in the most effective and efficient way, a systematic approach to marketing needs to be established. This systematic process will be organized in the form of a formal marketing plan. No marketing activities should be initiated without a plan. Unfortunately, the use in health and human services of the formal marketing plan is still relatively rare. In most health organizations marketing tends to be implemented on a piecemeal basis and is concentrated on public relations, advertising, and most recently, contracting. These health organizations rely on separate programs and plans whose coordination is often haphazard rather than synergistic.

The marketing plan specifies by service who will do what, where, when, and how, to accomplish the organization's goals in the most efficient method. The plan is a schedule of events and activities of a preplanned marketing effort. It outlines the marketing methods to be used, the resources to be committed, and the policy guidelines to be followed in achieving specific marketing goals and objectives.

POSITIVE OUTCOMES OF THE MARKETING PLANNING PROCESS

A marketing plan allows the health organization to:

— Evaluate the facility's existing marketplace;
— Evaluate the organization's marketing strengths and weaknesses;

— Identify the segments of the marketplace that should be served and marketed to by the organization;
— Penetrate a select segment of the marketplace;
— Capture a select target;
— Maintain a desired market share;
— Achieve key positioning/images within the community served;
— Lay a framework for new service development of existing service alteration;
— Identify specific strategies and tactics for the organization to implement;
— Satisfy the patient's needs in the marketplace; and
— Improve the financial viability of the health organization.

The marketing plan assists in identifying marketing opportunities, coordinates and unifies efforts to attract new patients, stimulates creativity within the organization, supports innovation as a planning by-product, encourages participation by all personnel within the organization, reduces costs with increased span of control, and allocates resources more efficiently.

BENEFITS OF MARKETING PLANNING

Planning does not assure performance, but it is a disciplined approach which can minimize failure. This is very important as most marketing programs in health organizations fail. In other words, they do not satisfy the majority of goals and objectives. Marketing planning is an allocation tool. The major goal of marketing planning is to achieve cost-effectiveness in marketing efforts and resources. This is the main reason why specific tasks are laid out systematically so that performance can be measured against the plan's objectives and goals.

The marketing plan is a communication tool between the health organization and the different groups with whom it serves and interacts. Marketing plans should be well-written documents so confusion and misunderstanding of functions and activities are eliminated. Effective communication with the organization's personnel and publics served can be obtained with a well thought-out marketing plan. In fact, someone unfamiliar with the organization should be able to read and understand the plan. This can lead to the plan's being effective over a long time frame. Marketing planning is an ongoing function which needs to be utilized throughout the existence of the organization. Paying attention to the marketing aspects of the organization can pay large dividends in relation to its marketing resource allocation being cost-effective.

PRELIMINARY STEPS TO WRITING A MARKETING PLAN

No marketing plan has ever been successful without a dedication and commitment to using marketing within a health organization. Thousands of marketing plans have been thrown into the "circular file" or sat on shelves collecting dust due to a lack of commitment by administration or the medical staff. A marketer must do the homework before ever writing a plan. In other words, they must market the function of marketing to management, staff, medical providers, and boards before developing and implementing marketing activities. Many marketers have wasted an enormous amount of time and energy due to this lack of preparation. Political and economic support for developing a marketing plan must be achieved before implementation. Superficial support, inadequate time to prepare a good plan, and poor implementation can undermine the potential cost-effectiveness of the planning process.

DEVELOPING A MARKETING PLANNING COMMITTEE

One of the most important steps in developing a marketing program is to create a marketing committee within the organization. This committee can provide excellent input from different perspectives and interests. It can also enhance the potential success and acceptance by all members of the staff, board, and medical staff. The key ingredient to a successful planning committee is the selection of the members of the committee. As an example, let us assume a marketing program is beginning to be discussed by a local community hospital. The minimum areas of the hospital which need to be represented on the committee are the board, executive director, director of patient or clinical care, director of planning, director of finance, chief of the medical staff, and director of marketing.

The committee must start out with the director of marketing having the executive director on the committee. It is essential to have the chief executive actively involved in issuing planning policies and giving approvals for action. The executive director should also be involved in developing a marketing subcommittee of the board of directors. Then a key member of the marketing subcommittee can be an active member of the marketing planning committee. Direct access and communication with the board and executive administration is vital for avoiding potential problems in the long run. The director of finance must be part of the committee for financial input and resource allocation decisions. The director of planning can provide coordination between the different planning and new service development activities going on in the organization. The chief of staff provides a key liaison with the medical providers. The director of patient care coordinates activities with the nursing staff and ancillary services. The committee, of course, can be greater in number than seven members. However, these seven members are essential for key representation. Also, a seven member committee is a good size for accomplishing a considerable amount in terms of decision-making. This first step to developing a marketing plan is necessary. It will be a major contributor to the potential success of the marketing planning process over the long-run.

THE MARKETING PLANNING PROCESS

As described in Chapter 1, there are four key sectors to the marketing planning cycle in health organizations. These four sectors include: ORGANIZATION, RESEARCH, CREATIVITY PROCESS, and CONTROL. These four phases of the planning process are interrelated throughout the planning cycle.

The key steps which will be described in the following chapters are listed below:

PLANNING PHASE	MARKETING ACTIVITY
ORGANIZATION:	Design of marketing function Marketing committee activities Development of marketing mission Establishment of marketing goals and objectives
MARKETING RESEARCH:	Review historical trends Develop an internal audit Develop an external audit

PLANNING PHASE	MARKETING ACTIVITY
	Analyze marketing opportunities and risks
	Identify segments and targets
	Establish positioning statements
CREATIVITY PROCESS:	Specific marketing strategies and tactics
CONTROL AND EVALUATION:	Create marketing budget and forecast
	Develop control system for performance evaluation
	Time line for implementation and control
	Refine goals/objectives

CONSTANTLY CHANGING ENVIRONMENT

It is quite evident that the health and human service industry will be experiencing significant changes through the next few years. Health policies are constantly being developed to contain costs, expand access, redirect us to preventive services, and alter the economic aspects of the marketplace. Most of the interest in health policy during the last twenty years has been related to allocating health services more equally, and most recently, improving their economic performance. The major emphasis of health policy currently is related to controlling the level of government involvement in health care and stimulating competition and free-enterprise in the marketplace.

Within this rapidly changing policy debate over cost-containment and marketplace characteristics, the health care industry has sought out new management tools to help direct them into the future. One of these key tools has been the use of marketing. The most important aspect of developing a marketing program for the health organization is the formulation of a marketing plan. The new emphasis on marketing is typical of industries which have been thrust into heavy competition, are worrying about survival, and are seeking the typical "quick cure" or "savior." Unfortunately, marketing is not a savior. It is only one management technique. The current and future direction of health public policy will enhance the importance of marketing in health organizations. The marketing plan can assist in lowering the incidence and risk of failure.

WHY MOST MARKETING PROGRAMS FAIL IN HEALTH ORGANIZATIONS

It is my estimate that the majority of marketing programs fail in health organizations. I have observed seven major factors which contribute to failures in marketing programs. If attention is paid to these key areas, there is a strong possibility that a reduction of risk in marketing will be achieved. These seven factors are:

1. LACK OF MARKETING PLANNING: As mentioned earlier, most health organizations still jump the gun and implement strategies without doing their homework in developing a formal marketing plan.

2. UNSOPHISTICATED TARGETING: Most marketers still use an undifferentiated or mass appeal approach to segmenting and targeting their potential patients or clients. Being more selective in differentiating to whom you are marketing can prove to be cost-beneficial. A select group of strategies needs to be developed for each target group. To increase the sophistication of targeting requires more attention to collecting marketing research information and analyzing the data.

3. LACK OF ADMINISTRATIVE AND FINANCIAL SUPPORT FOR MARKETING: As was mentioned earlier, the formulation of a marketing committee can prevent marketing programs from being sabotaged by boards, medical staff, or administrators who do not really believe in marketing and its benefits. In addition, marketing is not necessarily cheap. Enough financial resources must be allocated over a long time frame.

4. LACK OF COORDINATION BETWEEN DIRECTORS OF MARKETING, PLANNING, AND FINANCE: First of all, the position of marketing should be at a vice-presidency level within most health organizations. The position should have public relations, planning, fund development, and new service development reporting to it. In addition, there need to be excellent communication and working relationships between the director of marketing

and directors of planning or finance. The director of marketing should report directly to the executive director of the organization.

5. MARKETING DIRECTORS NOT POSSESSING ENOUGH TRAINING IN MARKETING: There are very few directors of marketing in health care with a broad range of knowledge about the wide scope of applications of marketing. Since the formal aspect of marketing has only been accepted within health organizations during the last decade it is easily understood why so few experienced marketers exist at this time. Most organizations assumed they could promote directors of public relations or planning to this function without exploring if they could adapt to the wider range of applications of marketing.

6. UNREALISTIC EXPECTATIONS: Marketing will not solve all the organization's problems, nor will it be a major success in a short time frame. Marketing is a management tool and must be adopted and implemented over a long time frame. An administrator must accept marketing as a key management tool, but only one to be integrated with finance, strategic planning, human resources management, economics, and policy analysis.

7. LACK OF INTERNAL MARKETING BEFORE IMPLEMENTING EXTERNAL STRATEGIES: A health organization must develop an internal marketing philosophy and mission. The staff must understand their roles within marketing the organization. Every staff member is a representative of the organization. Everyone markets the organization with every interaction. The organization must educate the board, medical staff, employees, administrators, and clinicians about marketing and direct them to play a role in marketing. The formal people who are affiliated with the organization are its greatest marketing resources.

These seven pitfalls can be avoided by paying attention to the marketing plan that is developed. Each of these reasons for failure can be avoided if the plan is thorough and pays attention to these problem areas.

NATURE OF STRATEGIC MARKETING PLANNING

Major changes are occurring in planning in health care organizations. This is indicated by the various ways in which planning is described, including: "business planning," "financial planning," "market planning," "strategic planning," "marketing planning," "strategic marketing planning," and other various combinations. These changes and variations are reflective of the fact that planning is becoming more "strategic" in nature. Planning is becoming more related to marketplace analysis, analyzing opportunities and risks, and laying a framework for new service development. This framework is forming a basis of strategy development as a key ingredient in all types of planning. Planning has shifted from a narrow functional area in an organization to encompass diversified, multi-service health organizations. The concept of the health organization as a collection of service units having various marketing objectives is at the foundation of current approaches to strategic marketing planning. The term portfolio is typically used to describe such a group of diversified services within one organization. This metamorphosis in planning is due to the fact that many health organizations are now confronted with limited financial resources due to rising costs of operation and limitations in reimbursement.

A strategic marketing plan is not the same, therefore, as a regular marketing plan. It is a plan of all aspects of an organization's strategies in a marketplace. This means that the financial, human resources, and policy planning aspects of the organization must be coordinated within the strategic marketing plan. This compares to a limited version of marketing planning which constrains itself to a select service and an individual marketing mix strategy. Effective strategic marketing planning is based on the premise that market opportunities have to be analyzed and the organization's capacity to take advantage of these opportunities requires assessment. The five major components of the foundation of strategic marketing planning are: CLIENTS OR PATIENTS, COMPETITORS, ENVIRONMENTAL TRENDS, MARKET CHARACTERISTICS, and INTERNAL STRENGTHS AND WEAKNESSES.

Strategic marketing planning is a natural outgrowth of the historical comprehensive health planning, financial planning, health systems planning, and more recently, operational strategic planning methodologies. It has evolved during recent times due mainly to the diversification and limited financial constraints which have materialized during the 1980s. A strategic marketing plan possesses the central theme that market opportunities differ in various markets. This requires every health organization to be strategically alert to take advantage of such opportunities in these diverse marketplaces. Strategic marketing planning has been aided significantly during recent years by computers and other technical processes. However, planning is a creative process which requires an extensive amount of creative strategic thinking by health managers.

The remainder of this book will address strategic marketing planning. It will be directed to developing a marketing plan for interrelating the health organization's future purpose, direction, and services with the organization's marketing missions, goals, and objectives. As mentioned earlier, the efficient allocation of marketing resources for achieving these goals and objectives will be the backbone of the planning process. It should answer a) where has the organization been?; b) what is our current business and purpose?; c) where do we want to be in the future?; and d) what do we need to do to become what we want our organization to be? By answering these questions, the health organization will be better able to deal with the contrivance of change, rather than just reacting to it. In today's ever-changing marketplace, action rather than reaction has to be the theme of future health management.

SUMMARY FOR CHAPTER 2: INTRODUCTION TO MARKETING PLANNING

One of the major reasons that many marketing programs have failed or not lived up to expectations has been the lack of the development of a formal written marketing plan. The marketing plan lays the framework from which we can market our services. Chapter 2 has provided some foundations about 1) what strategic planning is; 2) how it differentiates from strategic marketing planning; 3) the role marketing planning plays in the marketing process; 4) benefits of developing a marketing plan; 5) how to prepare for a marketing plan through marketing subcommittees and administrative support; and 6) key pitfalls to be aware of which have caused many marketing programs to end in failure.

Chapters 1 and 2 have provided background material for the reader to now progress into the key steps which need to be followed for the development of a successful strategic marketing plan. It is important to remember that the organizational structure of plans can vary but each of the planning components in the following chapters should be included in the process.

The next chapter discusses one of the most important steps in the marketing planning process—the creation of marketing missions, goals, and objectives.

CASE EXAMPLE FOR CHAPTER 2: STRATEGIC MARKETING PLANNING FOR HOME CARE SERVICES

The Home Care Marketplace

The home care business industry has received tremendous attention during the last couple of years due, especially, to the changes in Medicare's hospital payment plans. These reimbursement changes have created pressure to shift care from inpatient to less expensive alternative modes of care. Home care is one of the main beneficiaries of these changes. It is predicted by many that the home care industry will expand at a 20% annual rate from $4 billion in 1984 to over $15 billion by 1990. This growth is being fueled by: 1) the expanding market of population over the age of 65 which will reach 30 million by 1990; 2) creation of new diagnostic and preventive products which can be utilized in the home; 3) an intensified trend toward wellness and self-care; and 4) continued emphasis on more cost-effective modes of care.

The home care industry is not a homogeneous one. It consists of a broad array of various economic sectors. Each sector has its own marketplace, competition, and reimbursement methods. There are basically four sectors: sales or rental of home-care equipment, sales of diagnostic and self-care products, home visits by medical personnel, and sophisticated technology services such as dialysis. Over 75% of home care revenues is derived from home visits. Unfortunately, profits from this sector have been difficult to obtain. Insurance companies have been tight with coverage, especially for shift care, or 4-24 hours of constant care by nurses or nursing aides. Medicare and other third-parties have directed their coverage to short-term or intermittent home visits. Medicare, for example, typically pays at cost for care limited to sixty days of visits and treatments. Medicaid pays an amount less than cost. Private insurers often have a limit on a per diem basis. However, gradually insurance companies are experimenting with home care services as a potential cost-effective method for containing health care costs.

Hospital Economics Create Home Care Service Development

Hospitals have been facing extreme financial pressures and competition. The emphasis on strategic marketing planning for new service development is keen. Home care services appears to be an important growth area for many hospitals. Hospitals will represent a major provider of home care through the next few years even though proprietary home health agencies and skilled nursing facility-based home care organizations are currently growing at a greater rate. Over 1,000 hospitals around the country currently offer some form of home care services, with this expanding to over 2,000 by 1987. This expansion will not be easy as competition is fierce. Proprietary chains, hospitals, skilled nursing facilities, family service agencies, and community-based home care agencies are competing for a niche in the marketplace. In addition, prospective payment mechanisms for home care will apply to home care services within a couple of years. The DRG system currently being implemented is already impacting the home care industry with a sicker patient base, earlier hospital discharges, and greater use of intensive services. These changes offer greater marketing opportunities to the hospital-based programs. The incentive to develop home care programs is strong under the new Medicare rules that predetermine lengths of hospital stays for each type of illness. Home health care expenses are currently not subject to DRGs. Therefore, hospitals can maximize their earnings under the DRGs by discharging patients earlier and will not lose post-hospital revenue with the offering of home care programs. In addition, some types of costs can be shifted to separately organized hospital home care agencies and is allowed under Medicare rules. Hospitals are also allowed to add on a 13% on top of cost cap to cover the higher administrative costs incurred by a hospital-based home care agency compared to a freestanding agency.

A main reason for hospitals to get more involved in the home care marketplace is to ensure continuity and quality of care for the patient. By discharging a patient into a home care program, the hospital and physician can develop a longer-term treatment program. Unfortunately, many hospitals are adding on home care services as a potential method to make quick revenues. There is a faddish aspect to the development and cautious planning is required. This is especially true when competing with well-financed proprietary chains. For example, one of the world's largest hospital chains, Humana, recently entered the home care market with plenty of resources and expertise. Humana created a joint venture with Medical Personnel Pool to supply home care services for 68 of Humana's 90 hospitals around the country. The joint venture is for private pay patients only and Medicare is excluded. On the other hand, there are risks in the marketplace. For example, one of the largest private health companies in the country, Johnson and Johnson, recently decided to bail out of the home care business. J&J had been in the home care market since 1982 but had particular difficulty being successful in the Florida marketplace with its private Home Health Care, Inc. division.

All of these risks are part of the strategy planning process. Hospitals have evaluated the market attractiveness of the home care industry from the following strategic market planning factors:

— Market size
— Growth rate
— Relationship to alternative service development areas
— Level of competition
— Potential profit margins
— Potential for economies of scale
— Program quality
— Level of technology required
— Socio-demographic trends

These analysis areas allow the organization to establish a marketing strategic plan for entering the home care industry through the processes of our situational analysis, redesign of the organizational mission, establishment of marketing goals and objectives, creation of marketing tactics, and a control process.

Chapter 3

Organizational Phase: Setting the Stage with Marketing Missions, Goals, and Objectives

STEP ONE: ORGANIZATIONAL COMMITMENT

It is important to gain the support of the administration, medical providers, and board before beginning the development of a marketing plan. The level of support does not have to be unanimous, but it must be backed by key, politically based personnel. Too many marketing endeavors have been shelved or met with failure because of the lack of support by the main organizational personnel. This can be initiated by forming an organizational marketing committee and a marketing subcommittee of the board of directors. If the organization does not have an organizational board, a subcommittee of a community board might substitute. As mentioned in Chapter 2, the key representatives on the organizational marketing committee must be the executive director, a member of the board, director of patient or client services, director of finance, director of planning, and the director of marketing. In addition, before initiating a marketing plan some educational sessions about marketing for the board and key managers within the organization can prove cost-effective. Realistic expectations should be understood by these managers about the potential of the marketing program. Marketing will usually fail if it is a short-term function. It must be understood that a strong planning component has to be completed before initiating strategies and tactics.

STEP TWO: SET UP A STRATEGIC PLANNING CALENDAR

It needs to be understood that a typical planning process takes 3-4 months followed by a 8-9 month period of implementation for most kinds of health organizations. This would be followed by an evaluation, alteration, and refinement period of another year. Therefore, a new marketing department within a facility requires a minimum of two years before results are to be expected.

Planning activities must be scheduled with each activity. A basic schedule minimally includes PLANNING STEPS, ACTIVITIES INVOLVED WITH EACH STEP, SPECIFIC DATES, DESIGNATED RESPONSIBILITIES, and EXPECTED FOR COMPLETION. Again, this needs to be spread out over a 3-4 month planning period. This time frame is not unusual and allows for better safeguards without rushing into implementation. It also allows some time for educating the staff about marketing and gaining more organizational commitment and support. The planning calendar should be detailed and objective so deadlines and specific actions can be identified. A simplified typical calendar is presented below:

MARKETING PLANNING CALENDAR
FOR THE HEALTH CENTER

Planning Phase	Specific Activities	Dates
Organizational Phase	Develop Marketing Committee	Jan. 1-7
	Develop Marketing Missions, Goals, and Objectives	Jan. 7-30
Research Phase	Outline Marketing Audit	Feb. 1-15
	Complete Completion of Data	Feb. 15-March 15
	Analyze Audit-Targeting	March 15-30
Creativity Process	Develop Positioning	April 1-7
	Develop Strategies & Tactics	April 7-21

Planning Phase	Specific Activities	Dates
Control Phase	Develop Control System	April 21-30
	Develop Implementation Calendar	" "
Implementation Phase	Begins May 1st after completion of Four-Month Planning Calendar	

This marketing calendar requires agreement by the organizational marketing committee and board subcommittee. The development of the planning calendar is an excellent first activity for the organizational marketing group. However, the director of marketing should always be directing the organizational committee in order to provide accurate direction and insight into the marketing planning process. If a committee is not available the director of marketing and the director of planning can agree on the formal planning calendar. The executive director of the organization must have access to all planning information so that support is nurtured.

A MARKETING MISSION

One of the most important steps to writing a marketing plan is developing the organizational mission and the mission of the marketing plan. These mission statements are not necessarily the same. One will be describing the organization's purpose for existence and the other the marketing plan's purpose. Sometimes the mission step is overlooked or considered unnecessary. I have found that this step may be the most important one in the entire marketing planning process.

Organizational Mission Statement

The marketing mission lays the framework for the entire planning process. It basically describes the purpose and philosophy of the organization. The organizational mission statement should answer the following questions:

1. What business is the health organization in?
2. What is the purpose for the organization's existence in the marketplace?
3. Who does the organization serve?
4. What is the organization's culture?

Many organizational missions have not been attended to for many years. I have found, for example, that some religiously affiliated hospitals or clinics have not updated their missions for tens of years. Since marketplaces change constantly, missions of organizations also change. It is important that missions be refined and updated on a periodic basis.

Some of these questions are very difficult ones for administrators. For example, several administrators or board members have informed me after a thorough session that their health organization no longer has a useful purpose, or mission, within the community it serves. Some older clinics were developed during epidemics or earthquake periods to serve as emergency services. Their mission statements reflect this historical need. However, since that time an overcrowded marketplace has materialized and the same clinics have demonstrated that their services are duplicated throughout the community. However, the clinics have continued to serve a select public and in a definite mature phase or decline phase of their life cycle. In fact, I have even had executive directors in major metropolitan hospitals inform me that the only mission the hospital has is to financially support its employees and contribute economically to the local community. They indicate that their hospitals actually do not have a health purpose for their mission at this point in time.

However, most health organizations do possess a viable mission or purpose. The organizational mission statement should answer the prior four questions. The length of the organizational mission statement should not extend beyond two or three paragraphs. A sample mission statement for the marketing plan of a *local community hospital* might read:

> The . . . Community Hospital is a nonprofit community hospital which provides full-service inpatient and outpatient medical care. The . . . Community Hospital has provided care to the community residing in the southern quadrant of Crow County. For 50 years the hospital has provided the highest quality of care to meet the health needs of this population. Its staff is dedicated to the provision of medical services regard-

less of age, race, or income. The hospital strives to be sensitive and responsive to the complete health needs of the population through a well-managed organization. The hospital aims to improve the health status of the population served.

A second example would be the mission of a local *Family Service Agency*:

The Family Service Agency traces its roots to 1899 as a non-profit organization. The Agency is founded to: 1) prevent unnecessary use by clients of institutional care; 2) prevent dependency of clients on public welfare systems; 3) provide services to families under stress; 4) aid families to promote the physical, mental, and emotional development of their children; and 5) promote advocacy for the elimination of conditions that cause family life to deteriorate. The agency serves over 10,000 clients per year in 25 separate programs from all parts of the entire five counties.

A third example of an *army medical center*'s mission is:

To provide medical care to active duty military personnel and their dependents stationed in the Nevada area and to retired military personnel. It also provides medical education in various specialties to physicians and dentists in the military.

A fourth example for a *Health Maintenance Organization* is:

The HMO's mission is to maintain health care costs at an acceptable level to the health consumer; provide excellent health services on an IPA or HMO prepaid basis; stress preventive medicine by early detection and wellness, reinforce alternative modes of delivery; utilize less expensive ambulatory care services for the public; emphasize health education and behavior modification to raise the health status of the community; and provide easily accessible services to all members of the HMO within the community on a curative or emergency level.

A fifth example of a mission for a *nursing continuing education firm* is:

Continuing Education Services, Inc. is a for-profit nurse education organization which provides continuing education programs for nurses of all specialties within the local county boundaries. The firm is dedicated to presenting quality programs which are relevant to current clinical practices. The educational sessions are offered at convenient locations throughout the county in a practical approach by experienced practitioners and at affordable cost.

A final example of a mission is demonstrated for a *health insurance company*:

The XYZ Insurance Company operates as a non-profit corporation and as a member of the XYZ National Corporation to provide indemnity coverage for health, life, vision, and dental care. The organization offers other administrative services to the general public within the state, insurance professionals, agents, and brokers. The company is dedicated to the promotion of the member physician concept. The company seeks to maximize marketplace opportunities in order to provide the general medical consumer with lower costs and higher quality services.

All of these mission statements are written a little differently. However, they all attempt to demonstrate: 1) what business the organization is in; 2) what the organization's purpose for existence is; and 3) what its philosophy or culture is.

Mission of the Marketing Plan

Besides the organizational mission, a short statement should be developed answering WHAT IS THE OVERALL PURPOSE FOR DEVELOPING A STRATEGIC MARKETING PLAN? This mission allows us a macro-oriented direction toward the development of the actual plan. It lays the true basic framework for the planning process.

Some examples would be:

1. The mission of the marketing plan for the local community hospital is to recruit additional members of the medical staff and to improve relationships between the medical staff and administration.

2. The mission of the marketing plan for the Family Service Agency is to expand the network for fund raising for the agency in the community.
3. The mission of the marketing plan for the army medical center is to improve the community relations in the county with the center.
4. The mission of the marketing plan for the health maintenance organization is to increase enrollment and raise the level of utilization of health promotion within the local community.
5. The mission of the marketing plan for the continuing education firm is to make a viable profit for its owners.
6. The mission of the marketing plan for the insurance company is to increase its competitive position in the health insurance marketplace.

The organizational and marketing plan missions provide a base from which specific marketing goals and objectives can be developed.

IDENTIFYING MARKETING GOALS AND OBJECTIVES

Marketing goals and objectives are derived to assist in directing the strategic marketing plan toward its outcomes. Goals and objectives are the results we hope to achieve with the marketing program. As a differentiation, goals are the broad or macro-level outcomes we desire to achieve from the marketing plan. Marketing objectives are the specific or micro-level outcomes we hope to achieve and are associated with further defining a specific goal. Each goal lays the framework for developing objectives. A marketing goal is typically more generic and vague. Therefore, a MARKETING GOAL answers the question:

**What broad desired results do we want to achieve with our strategic marketing plan?

The MARKETING OBJECTIVES answer the question:

**For each goal, what are the specific outcomes we hope to achieve with the marketing plan?

*   *   *

For example, a marketing goal for the *family service agency* could be:

> **To improve access of counseling services to all members of the local community.

The marketing objectives would redefine the goal more specifically. For example, a marketing objective for the FSA could be:

> **To increase the number of new clients/month by 10%; or

> **To double the number of referrals from other social service agencies.

Goals and objectives must be reflective and consistent with the organizational and marketing plan missions.

*   *   *

As an example of a marketing *goal for the insurance company,* it could state:

> **To increase its marketshare.

The marketing *objective* could be:

> **To expand its current market share from 4% to 6% by the end of the year. Again, the objective further describes the goal and both are consistent with the mission of the plan.

*   *   *

An example of a goal for the *local community hospital* could be:

> **To recruit surgeons to the medical center.

A marketing objective related to this goal would be:

> **To add five internal surgeons to the medical staff of the center by August.

*   *   *

An example of a goal for the *continuing education firm* is:

**To make the organization's seminar division profitable after four years of losses.

The marketing objective for this goal would be:

**To incur a 3% profit margin from seminar revenues within the next fiscal year.

The examples demonstrate quantified marketing objectives. These objectives require an ability to forecast accurately a realistic numeric increase/decrease in a specific marketing goal. Most of the time goals and objectives are quantified by a consensus of the key planners and administrators involved in the marketing process. However, the margin of error can be significant if this process is not well attended to while writing a marketing plan. Since these goals and objectives can be modified after the completion of the environmental analysis, and while the plan is being modified, more accurate estimates will be established. In addition, since most marketers are a little too optimistic, it may pay to be a little conservative when establishing quantitative goals and objectives. This is also especially important as the goals and objectives will become the foundation for the evaluation and control phases of the marketing plan. After the marketer has thoroughly analyzed the internal and external environments of the organization, a more accurate estimate of quantitative outcomes of the plan can be organized. It may be important to have your marketing subcommittee make the final decision as to the accepted quantitative goals and objectives of the marketing plan through a consensus and brainstorming process.

*   *   *

The future steps of marketing research, targeting, and strategy development will be directed toward achieving these goals and objectives. Therefore, it is very important to define goals and objectives thoroughly and carefully. However, these goals and objectives are not fixed. They provide a direction for the collection of data in the marketing audit and must be flexible. After collecting data in the audit section of the plan some goals and objectives can be refined with the extra information. New goals and objectives may be added or old ones subtracted. Since these goals and objectives provide a rough path toward the rest of the planning process, it will be important to constantly refer back to the goals and objectives for evaluation and guidance.

By outlining the organizational and marketing plan missions, goals, and objectives, the plan has a direction. We begin to know what we want to achieve with our planning process for the health facility or program. It also provides a foundation from which to start designing our marketing audit and collecting marketing research data in step six. The typical strategic marketing plan varies in the number of marketing goals and objectives that are developed. A guideline that I have used is an average of four to five marketing goals and three to four marketing objectives for each goal. These goals and objectives will become a major part of our evaluation process at the end of the marketing plan in the control phase. The control system will be designed to periodically assess how effective the marketing program has been in achieving the marketing goals and objectives originally set up during this stage of the planning cycle. All of the marketing actions that are taken will be directed toward achieving these marketing missions, goals, and objectives.

SUMMARY FOR CHAPTER 3:
ORGANIZATIONAL PHASE:
SETTING THE STAGE WITH MARKETING MISSIONS,
GOALS, AND OBJECTIVES

In order to have some direction for the development of a marketing program, an initial step requires the creation of the purpose for the organization and the marketing plan, along with specific outcomes we hope to achieve with the plan. This is one of the most overlooked phases of marketing planning, yet it can be the most beneficial. These missions, goals, and objectives direct the development of the marketing audit, identification of targets we hope to market to, and the creation of specific marketing strategies and tactics for communicating to the most cost-beneficial target groups. In addition, when the plan is implemented the missions, goals, and objectives will play an important role in the control phase for evaluating the effectiveness of the marketing strategies and tactics.

Chapter 3 has provided the reader with 1) an applied description and differentiation of marketing missions, goals, and objectives; 2) an awareness that organizational commitment and support is essential for effective planning; and 3) an understanding of the usefulness of developing a marketing calendar as a guideline for the planning and implementation processes.

The marketing missions, goals, and objectives lay the framework for the selection of the kinds of data to be included in the marketing audit, as described in the next chapter.

EXAMPLE CASE SITUATION FOR DEVELOPING MISSIONS, GOALS, AND OBJECTIVES

CASE: MARKETING A HEALTH MAINTENANCE ORGANIZATION

Background

An HMO located in a suburban area of Detroit, Michigan began operations in 1980. The service area covered more than 180 square miles and encompassed a population of over 350,000. There were more than 3,000 employers in the area. The labor force was mixed with 25% being in manufacturing, 50% in nonmanufacturing, and the remainder in trade, transportation, and government. Unemployment was approximately 7%, with higher rates in the inner city areas. More than 75% of the area's physicians participated in the HMO which was well supported by the medical community. All physician members agreed to a reduced fee schedule for treatment of the HMO subscribers. The main competition consisted of two local Preferred Provider Organizations made up of small group practices and Blue Cross. The Blue Cross Plan had not been successful in reaching the level of desired subscribers. The HMO decided to develop a full marketing plan.

The initial step in developing a marketing program for the HMO was to identify the MISSIONS, GOALS, and OBJECTIVES. There lays the framework on which the rest of the marketing plan is constructed. The HMO management established the following missions, goals, and objectives:

ORGANIZATIONAL MISSION: The Detroit Plan is a health maintenance organization which provides health care through a prepaid health plan for the citizens of the Detroit, Michigan area.

MARKETING MISSION: The marketing program will entrench the Detroit Plan as the main health insurance alternative to Blue Cross in the community for the majority of businesses and unions.

GOALS AND OBJECTIVES:

Goal I: The marketing program will increase the HMO's market-share.

Objective I: To increase the HMO's market share from 5% to 10% by the end of the first year.

Goal II: To increase the number of businesses with more than 100 employees offering the HMO as an alternative to Blue Cross.

Objective II: To increase the number of companies with over 100 employees offering the HMO from 12 to 30 by June. This will be 30 out of a possible 44 companies with 100 or more employees.

Goal III: To have the HMO improve its image and perception in the minds of the Detroit consumers.

Objective III: To reduce the number of client complaints by 10% and increase the favorable response rate to the client questionnaire sent out after each client utilizes the HMO by 25%.

Of course, these goals and objectives are arbitrarily presented since the reader does not have access to the HMO's complete analysis. The exercise does point out the importance of 1) keeping the marketing mission directed toward steering the marketing plan toward the successful completion of its goals and objectives; 2) establishing the marketing goals in a simple manner with clarity, realism, and in broad terms; and 3) designing the marketing objectives to be concise, measurable, and reflective of the specific goal it further describes. These missions, goals, and objectives can lead us in an improved direction for the creation of the HMO's environmental analysis. The types of data included in this audit will be supportive of satisfying the marketing goals and objectives of the plan. The next chapter describes in greater detail the types of information which are included in an environmental analysis.

Chapter 4

Performing a Marketing Audit of the Health Organization's Environment

INTRODUCTION TO MARKETING AUDITING

Developing a marketing audit is similar to performing an environmental analysis, situational analysis, or marketing research. It is the collection of information about the health organization's external and internal environment. There are six main purposes for developing a marketing audit:

1. To collect general background information about the organization, its competitors, and its marketplace;
2. To identify key trends occurring in the external or internal environment;
3. To identify main strengths and weaknesses of the organization and its competitors;
4. To identify potential market opportunities for the organization to pursue and risks to avoid;
5. To provide a base from which to identify market segments and targets for the organization to potentially market to with a select and individualized marketing program; and
6. To provide a base from which to better understand the needs and behavior of the health consumer.

The marketing missions, goals, and objectives decided upon in the prior steps of the marketing plan provide a guideline to the types of data which require collection. The marketing audit has to be consistent with the missions, goals, and objectives of the plan. For example, if the main thrust of the plan is to recruit physicians to the staff, the marketing audit information will be related to this particular requirement. This consistency is important because marketing research data typically becomes overwhelming. Usually excessive information is collected. Marketing and health administration education tends to instruct excellent data collection and surveying techniques but emphasizes an excess of data collection. Therefore, the audit has to be streamlined to fit the type of organization we are marketing and within the boundaries of the plan's missions, goals, and objectives.

There is no question that detailed marketing information is critical to any marketing program today. Effective strategic marketing planning relies on a detailed, comprehensive evaluation of the organization's marketplace, the consumer's needs, the consumer's perceptions, and potential for growth. The marketing audit is basically an essential data base to guide the organization's positioning, targeting, and strategy development within the strategic marketing process. The well-defined marketing audit should allow the health organization to identify where intervention into the marketplace will do the most good for the organization and the health needs of the community.

COMPONENTS OF A MARKETING AUDIT

The marketing audit contains three main pieces of information: current behavior of the organization's markets, potential impact upon the marketplace from the organization's changing, and current and potential changes in causal factors. The information gathered will include data which can and cannot be controlled by the organization. Many pieces of information will not be impacted by the organization's decision to change.

The following MARKETING AUDIT provides an outline of the categories which are to be collected and systematically organized. This audit outline will be applied to a typical hospital, but is applicable to any type of health organization for generic informational categories.

Sample Marketing Audit

A good marketing audit will organize the data into two distinct groups: EXTERNAL and INTERNAL data bases. Within each of these two main groupings the data will also be systematically organized into distinct subcategories. It is important to cluster similar or related information into these categories for future analysis and easy reference. It is also necessary to identify a service area which the audit will be addressing. For example, a local hospital might limit its audit to the surrounding three counties or within a range of five square miles.

External Marketing Audit Information

Macroenvironmental Data:

ECONOMIC FACTORS: income levels, employment trends, inflation rates, unemployment rates, housing situation, poverty levels, industrial growth trends, interest rates on capital, energy prices and availability, health insurance coverage, and economic growth patterns in the community.

DEMOGRAPHIC FACTORS: population characteristics of distributions of age, sex, race, family size, household mix, area size, population growth and size, birth rates, death rates, health status, religious affiliation, transportation availability, and educational levels.

SOCIAL TRENDS: cultural activities, moral standards, recreational events, living standards and values, etc.

POLITICAL/LEGAL FACTORS: current and potential legislation affecting the specific service, lobbying trends; activities in antitrust, health, and safety, and environmental protection; political parties in office in local, state, and national government and their health directives; and consumer and special interests.

Microenvironmental Data:

MARKETPLACE FACTORS OF THE ORGANIZATION: current and potential demand for the service, size of current and potential market for service, economic structure of marketplace (competitive, oligopoly, monopoly, etc.), market share, current and future supply of similar services in the marketplace, etc.

COMPETITION: identification of similar and identical services in the community, strengths and weaknesses of the competition, estimate of future competition coming into the marketplace, needs and gaps in the marketplace, and reasons consumers use the competitors.

LOCAL HEALTH INDUSTRY: current status of medical technology in the area, changes in delivery modes, utilization trends, reimbursement trends, proprietary mix and intensity, distribution of providers, incoming and outgoing services and providers, and supplier availability for drugs or equipment.

CURRENT PATIENTS: number and identity of historical and current patients or clients; their addresses, telephone numbers, age, spouses, dependents, employers, occupations, insurance coverage, referral source, date of first and last contact, and attitude toward the service.

PSYCHOGRAPHIC/LIFESTYLE PROFILE: work and recreational habits of current patients and general population within service area; values, interests, attitudes, and perceptions toward the services and organization; purchasing habits of the service, loyalty status, and dates of when they were value programmed. Psychographics is discussed at more detail in a later section of this chapter.

MARKETING RESOURCES: historical and current marketing activities; historical planning or marketing research studies completed; administration support for marketing; relationships with board and medical staff; current staffing for planning, research, and public relations activities; and funding availability for marketing.

ORGANIZATIONAL STATUS: status of admissions, length of stay, average and standard deviation of daily census; utilization of ancillary and ambulatory services; number and mix of medical staff; effectiveness of triage system; patient waiting time; proportion of time understaffed or overstaffed; current services offered; occupancy rates; cost and revenue breakdown by service, revenue and expenditure contributions to other services; mix of Medicaid, Medicare, and private pay patients; fund raising activities; receivables rate; staffing patterns; and overall qualitative description of the organization's main strengths and weaknesses in the marketplace.

SOURCES OF INFORMATION
FOR THE MARKETING AUDIT

For all practical purposes the way in which the service area is defined will determine the type and amount of information that will be available for the marketing audit. The following general sources are available to find information classified within each category of the marketing audit which was previously described:

Sources of Information

Macroenvironmental Data:

ECONOMIC FACTORS: departments of commerce, labor, and census within the national and local governments; chambers of commerce; banks; brokerage houses; investment firms; planning agencies or commissions; local universities; business libraries, etc.

DEMOGRAPHIC: Department of Census, planning agencies, chambers of commerce, real estate firms, public and private libraries, local legislator offices, economic development agencies, transit authorities, etc.

SOCIAL: special interest groups, lobbying groups, church organizations, local newspapers, personal interviews and surveys, etc.

POLITICAL/LEGAL FACTORS: local legislators, congressional reports, newspapers, periodicals, lobbying groups, special interest groups, health and medical associations, etc.

Microenvironmental Data:

MARKETPLACE FACTORS: local health planning agencies, health consulting firms, investment firms, local public health agencies, Department of Health and Human Services, health and medical associations and consortiums, local health educational programs in universities, etc.

COMPETITION: phone directories, health and medical associations, health consulting firms, planning agencies, pharmaceutical and supply firms, departments of health, etc.

LOCAL HEALTH INDUSTRY: health and medical associations, health lobbying groups, labor unions in health, health marketing research firms, health consulting firms, health periodicals, planning agencies, state health regulatory agencies, local legislators, local newspapers, local medical center libraries, local research organizations, medical information centers and talk lines, proprietary chains, interviews and surveys, etc.

CURRENT PATIENTS: administrative and medical records, phone directories, census tracts, zip code directories, industrial employment directories, local department of records, health insurance companies, franchise tax boards, state departments of health, boards of equalization, local health systems agencies, and surveys.

PSYCHOGRAPHICS: consumer surveys or focus groups, interviews, patient surveys, discharge surveys, research firms, etc.

MARKETING RESOURCES: interviews with board members, administrators, current marketing personnel, directors of finance and planning, budgets, etc.

ORGANIZATIONAL STATUS: medical records, utilization reports, financial statements, interviews with administrators, etc.

All of the marketing audit information needs to be accumulated from a wide mix of different sources. However, a considerable amount of data is typically already available internally from the patient or client record, consulting reports already completed, interviews with appropriate personnel, and financial and utilization reports. Do not overlook the client or patient record or the local telephone directory. They can provide some of the most useful sources of information. However, to make things simpler, marketing research firms are usually available in local cities to perform a major portion of the audit if money and time allow. These firms, for example, can provide low-cost demographic profiles of any sized market. These profiles typically consist of converted census bureau information tapes condensed into short reports. They can show population, number of households, average family size, racial distribution, age distribution, per capita income, average family income, and average household income covering anywhere from a few blocks radius to several miles.

In addition, personal and mainframe computers can be a great aid to the marketer. For example, since 1980 there have been hundreds of software programs available specifically to assist in marketing research. These programs allow for easy input into structured outlines for data collection. Others even perform some basic analysis work in clustering commonalities and trends for targeting purposes. The time is approaching for the health marketer to not have to spend that much time on the collection of information for the marketing audit. There are key software directories available for all purposes in health marketing. The personal computer is revolutionizing the function of marketing research and analysis.

Marketing research is becoming more sophisticated in health care. Research budgets and staff have expanded significantly. Marketing research is now being used for new service development, targeting, image improvement, cost-containment, resource allocation, competitor analysis, understanding consumer behavior, and strategic planning. The sophisticated techniques include the use of focus groups, computer software packages, telemarketing surveys, mail questionnaires, videotex systems, and mapping processes. Just over fifteen years ago marketing research was unknown to most health organizations. Today, health organizations are beginning to use marketing research with considerable frequency and higher levels of sophistication.

NEWER RESEARCH TECHNIQUES: FOCUS GROUPS, TELEMARKETING, AND VIDEOTEX SYSTEMS

FOCUS GROUPS have been used to gather information by marketing research firms for many years. Health care has only recently started using them as a marketing tool. The concept is that of assembling a small group of former or potential patients or clients for an in-depth discussion of their reactions to the health organizations, services, or staff. Consumer goods marketers have long used focus groups to investigate deeply into the feelings that mass surveys cannot cover. Consensus is that focus groups are highly useful assuming that they are used with surveys, patient representatives, and other quality assurance tools. An example of a specific focus group would be a hospital surveying some former patients about the quality of care they received at the hospital. The key ingredients of the process include picking patient groups by type of treatment, i.e., former hysterectomy patients, and length of stay; limiting the number of the focus group to about 8 to 10 people; meeting with them in an informal living-room atmosphere; videotaping the sessions for future reference; limiting the session to about 1 to 1½ hours; making sure the patient's doctor is informed; and having a trained quality assurance expert present for the session. Led by an interviewer, the focus group provides information about the hospital's services but not necessarily direct and specific answers. Small samples such as two or three focus groups from the target market are usually sufficient to provide an indication of the value of various concepts or strategies to be tested. Focus groups can be an excellent tool for collecting information about consumer attitudes, values, interests, and perceptions. The purpose of a focus group is to determine what is important to them, what is unimportant, and how they make a purchase in a select service area. Often, the focus group mixes users of one service or organization with users of another or competitive service. The attempt in that case is to learn why health consumers using one service are different from consumers of competitive services.

This process also helps to identify what they consider to be the key benefits from a particular service. Generally, focus groups only provide broad, general ideas or directions that may be pursued through other forms of quantitative or qualitative research.

TELEMARKETING is another tool which is beginning to finally be used by health marketers. Telemarketing is a form of using the telephone or computer to make contact with the health consumer or provider. With the advent of Wide Area Telephone Service (WATS) lines, interviewing throughout the country can now be done from any hospital or health organization in any part of the country. Traditionally, the access to people came from patient records or telephone directories. Now the computerized random digit dialing makes any connected telephone a potential part of the survey. Telephone interviews are excellent for gathering a small amount of information from a large number of people. Since contact is by voice, questions must not require visual aids or thorough understanding of complex topics by the interviewees. A telephone interview may last 10-15 minutes with many close-end questions, that is, questions for which a list of answers is provided. Surprisingly, telephone respondents may actually provide more information or be more honest than in-person interviews. Consumers tend to be more open since the telephone becomes the defense mechanism for anonymity. Telephone interviews do have some disadvantages. For example, answers must be shorter and not as in-depth as those obtained in other methods. There is no opportunity to use any visual aids or props. However, these disadvantages are minimal in comparison to the strong cost-benefit aspects of comparing personal versus telephone interviews. Because of its low cost, high response rate, and small time requirements, the telephone survey is often the best method to use in surveying the general community.

VIDEOTEX is an interactive electronic system in which data and graphics are transmitted from a computer network over telephone or cable lines and displayed on a subscriber's TV or computer-terminal screen. There are about twenty-five private videotex firms in the country which contract with subscribers to the service. These firms provide programs such as news, sports, finance, at-home banking, travel information, games, education, directories, security scanning, and medical emergency monitoring. Marketing research firms see videotex systems as a major consumer auditing tool for the future. On the research side, surveys can be done directly to consumers through the personal computer. The American consumer is becoming more computer literate. As households continue to add computers to their possessions, the health industry will be better able to survey consumers directly and instantaneously through a videotex system. The industry can also use the system as a key educational tool for self-diagnosis, preventive health, and for marketing their specific services. Videotex systems are currently used sporadically in health organizations, but the potential and outlook is for much greater utilization of this effective marketing tool. The future of improving marketing techniques in health care will be related to making better use of the telecommunication technology that is already available.

Other forms of typically used marketing research techniques include direct observations, personal interviews, mail surveys, and consumer panels. Since the costs of marketing research continue to spiral, mechanisms which provide a leveraged or multiplier impact are being utilized more frequently. This means that more people need to be contacted in the shortest amount of time and at the least cost. This again puts the emphasis on telemarketing, mail surveying, and group sessions. Large amounts of information can be gathered through a mail survey. Respondents tend to give more thorough answers since the interview is anonymous. Since no one is there to provide guidance to the questions, the questionnaire form must be made as easy as possible to follow with primarily close-ended questions. Data gathering by mail is relatively inexpensive. The main costs are for the mailing lists, the questionnaire forms, and postage. Mail questionnaires ordinarily have a fairly low return rate. A 30 to 40 percent response to a mail questionnaire is considered normal. Obtaining a return of 60 to 70 percent is exceptional. All results depend, of course, on the service interest, quality of the questions, and the accuracy of the mailing lists. Mailing lists can be purchased directly from research and consumer behavior firms in local cities.

SUMMARY FOR CHAPTER 4: PERFORMING A MARKETING AUDIT OF THE HEALTH ORGANIZATION'S ENVIRONMENT

Marketing research, auditing, environmental analysis, and situational analysis are generally synonyms for the functions of collecting and analysis of historical and current information about a health organization's environment. With the marketing missions, goals, and objectives providing a base, the collection of marketing research data has gradually become easier with the development of personal computers and auditing software. Today, the majority of basic demographic, economic, and select aspects of market analysis information can even be purchased from marketing research firms.

Unfortunately, the availability of key data is still scattered among many different sources. However, with a quality marketing research software program, the organization and systematic collection of the data can be improved.

Chapter 4 has provided the reader with 1) the differentiation between macro- and microenvironmental data; 2) key sources for collecting information for the audit; and 3) a systematic framework for organizing the marketing audit.

The main purpose of the collection of this information is to be able to analyze the marketplace and identify market opportunities, potential risks, and lay a framework for segmenting and targeting the marketing programs. From the audit analysis key gaps in the marketplace for our services will surface and a framework for prioritizing the targeting process materializes. The next chapter discusses the nuts and bolts of segmenting and targeting in the marketplace based on the information aggregated and analyzed in the marketing audit.

CASE EXAMPLE:
MARKETING RESEARCH FOR AN INDEPENDENT
PRACTICE ASSOCIATION (IPA)

CENTURY PROTECTION was established as an independent practice association in 1982 to help serve the health needs of the Tampa, Florida community. The mission of the IPA is to encourage efficient and quality delivery of health care while controlling costs at the local and state levels.

There are currently fifty physicians of all specialties as partners in Century Protection. The key to the IPA program is the protection of the client-physician relationship. Each client can choose a primary care physician from among the participating physicians.

Century Protection is currently seeing 3,000 clients within the Tampa area. The board of directors of Century Protection desires to increase this enrollment by 300% during the next two years with the assistance of a formal marketing plan. As part of the marketing plan, it is necessary to examine the local community, the IPA's marketplace, and internal environment. This is the process which will allow the IPA to focus its resources on overcoming environmental constraints and taking advantage of marketing opportunities. It also will allow for a more sophisticated segmenting and targeting process.

The Board of Directors hired a marketing research firm to complete a marketing audit of the IPA's external and internal environments.

Some environmental conditions identified by the audit that may affect IPA development include:

Macroenvironmental Information:

Economic Factors: From Department of Commerce and Labor

— Average household income—$23,000
— Local unemployment rate—7%
— Percentage of Population Under Poverty—10%
— Local inflation rate—6.5%
— Industrial Growth—large semiconductor industry development in Southwest part of town
— Health insurance coverage—89% of current population possesses some form of health insurance

*   *   *

Demographic: From Department of Census

— Average age of population—31
— Average Family Size—4 members
— Public transportation—good bus and rail transportation
— Birth rate trend—up 23% during last ten years
— Minority proportion of population—48%

*   *   *

Social Trends: From local newspapers, churches, social clubs

— Conservative political area
— Consumer-oriented—retail sales very strong
— Population values preventive health
— Strong religious groups

Political/Legal: From local board of supervisors, mayor's office, legislative reports

— Strong lobbying for minorities
— Very conscious about environment
— Considerable number of health special interest groups concerned with the cost of health care
— Movement toward greater participation of business-health coalitions

Macroenvironmental Information:

Marketplace: From personal surveys, department of planning, local medical association, local hospital association and council

— Highly competitive environment with many physicians and group practices with more moving into the area
— Current marketshare of approximately 5%
— Market structure in monopolistic competition

*   *   *

Competition: From consumer and patient surveys

— Three other IPAs in the area
— 12 Group practices competing directly with this IPA
— Major weakness of other three IPAs is the fact that patients cannot choose their own physician

*   *   *

Local Health Industry: Industry reports from local associations, councils, state agencies, planning commission, newspapers, etc.

— Health system is moving toward greater ambulatory services such as same-day surgery, outpatient care, home services, etc.
— Strong movement into the area by large proprietary hospital chains such as Humana and Hospital Corporation of America
— Higher deductibles for local Medicaid and Medicare reimbursement

Patient Profile: From current and historical patient records

— 3,000 current patients
— all addresses, ages, employers, occupations, insurance coverage, source of referrals, etc.

* * *

Psychographic/Lifestyle: From household surveys

— athletic population—jogging, tennis and golf are popular
— perceive the Century services as excellent overall
— loyal clients
— visit their Century physician regularly

* * *

Marketing Resources: From internal analysis and records

— no marketing director
— physicians willing to allocate 1% of revenues to marketing
— most physicians still do not believe in marketing or have a misconception that marketing is only advertising

* * *

Physician Profile: From member resumes and physician telephone survey

— Average age—50
— Equal mix of specialties and none excluded
— geographically located within three mile radius
— Most dedicated to IPA being successful, some dissension with board

* * *

This information can lead the marketer to finding market opportunities to pursue and risks to avoid. As discussed in the next chapter, the audit can assist in segmenting and targeting their marketing programs more effectively.

Chapter 5

Segmenting and Targeting
the Marketplace

INTRODUCTION TO MARKET SEGMENTATION
AND TARGETING

It has only been during recent years that health organizations have started to pinpoint their potential patients/clients with more marketing sophistication. The subdividing of a marketplace into distinct sections is known as segmenting. The evaluation and selection of those segments which appear to be the most cost-beneficial is called targeting. Health care organizations need to segment and target effectively in order to develop more appropriate services and improve their communication network with their clients and patients.

Segmenting a marketplace is similar to cutting a pie into many different pieces. Each piece becomes a market segment which can be addressed by the health care organizations. Traditionally, segmenting a marketplace was directed toward mass appeal. Health care attempted to be all things to all people. Unfortunately, resource constraints prevented us from being able to serve all of the health needs of society. This has led administrators to be more selective in allocating their resources and to differentiate their services within the community to select population groups, or targets. As competition grew differentiation by physical features, quality of service, mode of delivery, style, or image became more important in marketing health services.

From the marketing audit information gathered, potential groups which could be marketed to, or segments, can be identified. The maximum number of segments is the total number of publics in the marketplace. However, as mentioned before we need to be more selective to whom we intend on marketing our services. The act of evaluating, selecting, and concentrating on those segments that the organization can serve most effectively is MARKET TARGETING. Any segment could be selected as a market target to be reached by a distinct marketing mix.

FACTORS FROM WHICH SEGMENTS CAN BE SELECTED

The marketing audit supplies the background data and trends to be able to identify the "laundry list" of segments which could be marketed to by the health organization. After we select this laundry list of all potential groups or individuals which could be marketed to, a selection will be made of primary and secondary targets. These targets will be the most promising or cost-beneficial segments which should be addressed initially by the marketing plan.

The segments are typically chosen by grouping key data classifications or trends. Segmenting a marketplace has typically been accomplished by the following boundaries:

GEOGRAPHIC VARIABLES, i.e., regionalization, city size, county size, density, climate, etc.;

DEMOGRAPHIC FACTORS, i.e., age, sex, family size, educational level, racial breakdown, population growth rates, family size, etc.;

ECONOMIC FACTORS, i.e., occupation, labor force mix, income levels, wealth, consumption habits, poverty levels, insurance coverage, etc.;

SOCIAL FACTORS, i.e., religion, nationality, cultural aspects, political philosophy, social class, etc.; and

PSYCHOGRAPHIC/LIFESTYLE VARIABLES, i.e., individual values, interests, opinions, personality traits, habits, athletic activities, work, stress levels, recreational hobbies, behavioristic aspects of purchasing services, loyalty status to service, perceptions of services, awareness level of service, etc.

EXAMPLES OF SEGMENTS

As an example, potential segments for various types of health organizations are listed below:

Preventive Dentistry Practice: financial district workers, upwardly mobile adults, business travelers, shoppers, families, etc.;

Health Maintenance Organization: labor unions, corporate employees, families, young adults, etc.;

Community Hospital: general population, physicians, local human service agencies, government agencies, media, planning agencies, etc.;

Nursing Home: senior adults, families, hospital discharge planners, physicians, gerontology programs, community senior care programs, etc.;

Same-Day Surgery Center: two-income families, physicians, local hospitals, family service agencies, corporate employee benefit directors, etc.;

Preferred Provider Organization: physicians, hospitals, clinics, general population, insurance companies, etc.; and

Executive Stress and Wellness Program: corporate executives, commuters, benefit directors, holistic health centers, athletic clubs, etc.

All of these segments could become target groups to which marketing strategies are implemented.

PRIORITIZING THE SEGMENTS INTO TARGET GROUPS

Once the segments of a marketplace have been identified, the targeting or segment prioritizing process begins. Targeting attempts to pick out primary and secondary individuals or groups from our list of market segments which the health care organization needs to communicate with through a defined marketing program. Targeting has mainly used the following approaches:

UNDIFFERENTIATED TARGETING—attempts to market services to a mass audience and to as many different market segments as possible;

DIFFERENTIATED TARGETING—attempts to market the service to several market segments with a common denominator of characteristics; and

CONCENTRATED TARGETING—emphasizes marketing to a select segment within the senior marketplace.

The market segments are divided into primary targets which have the greatest cost-benefit ratio and potential return, and secondary targets which may require attention as back-up or long-term consideration. It is recommended that the health care organization concentrate on a few select target groups for their marketing programs. Mass marketing in an overcrowded marketplace has proven not to be the most cost-effective method of targeting for health services.

Of course, many factors will contribute to limiting the number of segments selected for the marketing program. For example, organizational resources such as the available capital to invest into marketing activities or marketing talent of the staff; homogeneity between services; the stage of the life cycle in which the service is operating; or the homogeneity of the consumers in terms of the commonality of their tastes, preferences, amounts purchased, and reactions to market changes may limit the number and type of target groups to be addressed by a marketing program.

A good guideline to use is to derive a minimum list of *twelve segments* for the marketing plan; *three to four primary targets*; and *two to three secondary targets*.

SPECIFIC EXAMPLE OF TARGETING: AFFLUENT PRIVATE-PAY CLIENT

One of the most common target groups for health organizations during recent years has been the affluent sector of the population. The affluent market has quadrupled in size since 1975 and is growing much faster than any other. As restrictions have been placed on Medicaid and Medicare reimbursement, it has been typical for group practices, clinics, human service agencies, and hospitals to direct their attentions to attracting a higher share of private-pay clients. These private-pay patients typically are covered by private health insurance. Therefore, the first criteria was to identify all of the population within the marketplace which has private insurance. The second criteria might be the income level of this insured group. For example, the high level affluent group has been described as those earning more than $45,000 per year. There are, for example, over 26 million adults in this segment, or about 10% of all adults and 7% of all households in the country. All in all, this is a very rich and active market. These are the people who have the means of affording innovative and expensive new health services. The affluent group has three times more income and eleven times more discretionary spending power than the rest of the population. A third criteria could be household size. For example, two-thirds of these affluent adults who possess private health insurance live in households where more than one person earns an income. And half of them have children under the age of eighteen. Some additional criteria would be the sexual mix, educational level, marital status, and geographical location. For instance, this group includes 54% males, 73% with a college education, 90% being married, and they reside in all geographic regions of the country in fairly equal numbers. Other potentially important information about this group could be the fact that nearly all affluent adults have one or more major credit cards, consume 3½ times as much alcohol per household as the non-affluent, and spend four times as much on health-related products and services as the non-affluent. All of these variables assist in narrowing the target group to a micro-level. The organization can then begin to develop a specific plan of action, or strategy, to communicate with this select target group.

SECOND EXAMPLE OF TARGETING: SENIOR CARE MARKET

Many health organizations are beginning to pay attention to the senior care marketplace. The dimensions of long-term and senior care services being developed are rooted in the demographic changes of our society. For example, one in every five Americans will be 65 years of age or older by the year 2030 as the baby boom generation ages and life expectancy grows. Today, there are 30 million people over age 65. The enormous demographic shift crossed a watershed in 1983 when for the first time in American history, people over 65 outnumbered teenagers. This maturing of the American population has increased the dollar value of the consumer marketplace for the mature population to over $400 billion a year. In order to target this group in a community the variables of age, income levels, geographic location, attitudes toward health services, size of household, lifestyle, home environment, current health status, and their insurance coverage have to be combined. The marketing plan must narrowly define this sector of the population and then develop a specific strategy to attract them to the service.

INTERMARKETING

Sometimes market segmentation and targeting can become too selective where the health care administrator is possibly missing important secondary and tertiary audiences. A targeting method for attempting to reach several different target groups at the same time is called the multiplier effect or intermarketing. Intermarketing allows the administrator/marketer to look at their total markets. It is like dropping a pebble in a pond. The first ring is your primary target market with the following concentric rings being your secondary and tertiary targets. The most common intermarketing channels are television, newspapers, and other ad vehicles which reach a general interest audience. For example, an advertisement in a long-term care trade publication may target administrators or medical providers in long-term care. However, an ad in a select newspaper may not only reach the administrator/medical provider but other human service administrators, families in the community, and other professionals. The intermarketing concept can coexist with concentrated targeting. Intermarketing attempts to reach all of the various, narrowly defined target groups that make up your patient/client base. For example, senior care products have long used generic media channels such as *TV Guide* to reach the grandparents within a household as the primary target. The ad then reinforces their product in the minds of the parents as the secondary target and their children as a tertiary target. If the service or product is not too selective then intermarketing may be a good marketing strategy. However, many health care services and products will be marketed more effectively by concentrated targeting.

It is important to research, segment, and target your marketplace for your services. Think your way through the whole marketing program before selecting the most appropriate media channel. Targeting will take some extra time, but may reduce the margin of error in implementing marketing programs.

USING CONJOINT AND CLUSTER ANALYSIS IN TARGETING

As the number of health services continues to saturate the marketplace, it is becoming more important to use a consumer-oriented targeting approach. One tool is conjoint analysis which assists the marketer in finding out which service features are more important to consumers and why. For example, select segments of the population may be motivated to use a service based on their availability of advisory service, friendly staff, low prices, or greater access to the service. By surveying consumers as to their preferences and clustering consumers into groups with similar tastes and preferences, a more sophisticated targeting approach can be developed. Once the segments are identified, they can be compared for differences in demographic composition, purchasing power, loyalty to a select service, and other variables. From this clustering process the target group with the highest potential for usage of the services can be identified.

A conjoint approach to targeting includes the following steps:

1. Identifying important attributes of the service which are important among alternatives which are potential targets.
2. Profiles or descriptions of alternative services including these valued attributes are developed.
3. Each potential target group is asked to indicate his/her preferences for the service attributes described in step 2.
4. The people with similar preferences are then clustered together to form narrower targets.
5. These narrowly defined targets with similar attribute preferences can then be marketed to more effectively.

Conjoint analysis attempts to allow the marketer to better understand the consumer and match their services. A similar concept to improving their understanding of the potential target group is Psychographic and Lifestyle Analysis which is described in the next section. At this point in the marketing plan, the marketer or administrator will have identified their most cost-beneficial target groups. After a little more refining through a better understanding of their values and interests, specific strategies and tactics can begin to be developed for each select target group.

USING PSYCHOGRAPHICS AND LIFESTYLE ANALYSIS FOR TARGETING

One of the main reasons why the majority of marketing programs fail in health care is the lack of sophisticated market segmentation and targeting. Marketers have long used demographic characteristics for estimating a consumer's potential utilization of a service. Most of these analyses are based on "who" and "what" characteristics rather than "why" clients use health services. Understanding the "why" component has led to the development of psychographic/ lifestyle analysis. Psychographics may be viewed as the practical application of the behavioral and social sciences to marketing research. It seeks to describe human behavior characteristics of clients/patients in their lifestyle, attitudes toward health services, interests and opinions, and personality traits and perceptions of the service's attributes.

Components of Psychographics

Psychographic/lifestyle analysis can be broken into four main divisions:

I. *Psychological attributes:* This area answers the basic questions: a) What kind of an individual is a client?; b) How do clients perceive themselves?; and c) Why do clients do the things they do? Most of these attributes are related to personality traits such as the patient's being: aggressive, gregarious, ambitious, creative, risk-taking, passive, competitive, etc. Many preconceptions about health services are derived from these attributes. For example, the stereotype "only the old segment of the population uses nursing homes" is derived from these types of attributes.

II. *Lifestyle variables:* Lifestyle attributes relate to the method in which people allocate their time for themselves or their families. Some lifestyle variables include: sexual preferences, athletic activities, work habits, daily routines, travel, and even cultural endeavors.

III. *Behavioristic or purchasing variables:* These attributes evaluate a person's purchasing habits of health care services. A person can obtain a health service based on their: a) regularity of purchase; b) user status; c) loyalty strength; d) level of need; e) benefits of service perceived; and f) motivation for utilization. Understanding these habits, for example, can allow for strategies to be developed related to enhancing referrals.

IV. *Service attributes and perceptions:* The last area is how people perceive the services related to psychological or physical characteristics. For example, price and value aspects are the foundation for the question, "Are these trips worth the weekly trips to the Ambulatory Care Center?"; and quality is the basis for the comment, "Only the best physicians are associated with this ambulatory care center."

Reasons for Using Psychographics

The use of psychographic/lifestyle analysis can allow the administrator to:

1. Identify select market segments or targets for which to develop individualized marketing programs;
2. Restimulate existing senior services which are being underutilized;

3. Become better able to identify client needs, and thus, matched services; and
4. Strengthen the financial viability of the long-term care organization and serve their clients/patients cost-effectively.

Examples of Psychographic/Lifestyle Services

Some examples of health services which have been developed during recent years related to their psychographic/lifestyle foundation are:

1. *Sport-Care Programs* based on athletic lifestyle;
2. *Alcohol Rehabilitation Programs* related to lifestyle;
3. *Meals On Wheels Programs for the elderly* related to the non-mobile senior citizen;
4. *Wellness Programs* related to changes in values and perceived benefits from traditional forms of care;
5. *Stress Management Programs* related to work habits;
6. *Ambulatory Senior Services* related to new acceptance of alternative forms of care and cost consciousness; and
7. *Pain Management Programs* related to new awarenesses of treatment procedures.

Psychographic/lifestyle and demographic information can complement each other. Demographics can describe the physical attributes while psychographic/lifestyle information can analyze the psychological and emotional aspects of the health consumer. In this way the health care manager can specifically pinpoint target groups, better understand why people use certain services, and be able to create marketing strategies for each selective target group. Each marketing strategy can be organized to meet the needs indicated in the psychographic/lifestyle profile. In other words, the marketing mix components of product, price, place, and promotion can be specifically designed to meet the psychographic needs of the consumer.

SUMMARY FOR CHAPTER 5:
SEGMENTING AND TARGETING THE MARKETPLACE

The marketing missions, goals, objectives, and audit have provided background information for the identification of select groups, individuals, or organizations to which the health organization needs to market its services. Chapter 5 provides the reader with 1) a differentiation between segmentation and targeting; 2) a methodology for selecting segments and targets; 3) multiple examples of targeting; 4) a review of conjoint and cluster analysis; 5) the importance of intermarketing in the targeting process; and 6) a thorough analysis of the use of psychographic and lifestyle analysis used in targeting services.

Market targeting has been accomplished rather haphazardly. Unsophisticated targeting has also led to raising the level of risk involved in implementing marketing programs for health organizations. In a competitive marketplace and with tremendous organizational pressures to be effective in our marketing programs, spending some time on formulating a differentiated or concentrated approach to targeting has proven to be cost-beneficial in the long-run.

From this step in our marketing plan we have now identified the most promising groups to direct our marketing programs to in the community. However, before we start developing specific strategies and tactics there is a need to understand how we want to position the services. The next chapter explores market positioning the organization and its services in the minds of the target groups that were identified in this chapter.

CASE EXAMPLE:
MARKET SEGMENTATION AND TARGETING
FOR A LOCAL FAMILY SERVICE AGENCY

The Family Service Agency provides counseling and support services to adults and children throughout the community. Most of the mental health programs are provided to select target groups. This segmentation process can be described by the following:

SERVICES	TARGET
Ombudsman Program	Volunteers for assisting nursing home administrators as legal advocates. *This can be undifferentiated as the entire general adult community can be targeted as volunteers.*

SERVICES	TARGET
Respite Program	Adults who can leave their children for a day or night to prevent potential child abuse. *This is more of a differentiated target as all adults do not meet these standards or need these services—only parents with young children typically will be marketed.*
Crisis Line	Adults who are at points of high stress which might cause abuse to children. *This is a differentiated target as only adults with children will be marketed to.*
Mothers' Group	Married parents who desire training and support in bringing up their children. *This is more of a concentrated target as the service is concentrating on married parents.*
Black Family Program	Young, black, upwardly mobile families for mental health services related to their unique needs. *This is a differentiated target as we are targeting by race, age, and income level.*
Naval Family Program	Navy families for mental health support services living on the local naval base. *Differentiated targeting by occupation, geographic location, residence, marital status, and size of family.*

SERVICES	TARGET
Developmental Disability Program	Children between the ages of 10-17 for support services who are physically disabled. *Differentiated target by being a child, age, and location.*
Single Parent Program	Single parents who desire support as a single parent and in bringing up their children. *Concentrated target on just young single parents living within a select radius of the agency.*
High School Teen Program	Teens who want to participate in getting academic credit for taking care of senior citizens from five local high schools. *Target is differentiated by age, school, values, and social consciousness.*
Senior Day Treatment	Senior citizens for support services in socialization. *Targeting by age, geographic location, and values.*
Teenage Pregnancy Program	Teens up to 18 years of age for self-pay parenting, nutrition, etc. programs. *Targeting by age, location, income level.*
Family Development	Handicapped children for support and development programs. *Targeting by physical ability, families of handicapped, and age.*
After care	Services for the chronically mentally ill and their families. *Targeting by geographic location, degree of illness, families of handicapped.*

SERVICES	TARGET
Foster Grandparents	Seniors to assist in taking care of children. *Targeting by age, location, mobility, and values toward children.*
Senior Companion	Seniors able to be a companion to other seniors. *Targeting by age, ability to travel, and values toward other seniors.*
Japanese Mental Health	Mental health counseling services for the Japanese adult population. *Targeted by nationality, age, and location.*
Child Care Center	Day care services for children. *Targeting by occupation of adults, marital status, age of children, etc.*

All of these services provide an example of differentiated and concentrated targeting related to special services. These target groups can be prioritized according to the importance of the select service to the agency and the potential for effectiveness. For example, the agency may have just received funding from local foundations for some of the programs. These programs may then receive top priority as they will lay the groundwork for future funding patterns. Other criteria may be the proportion of total revenues which each program contributes to the agency, interests of the board of directors, influence by the local United Way Agency, and abilities of the counseling staff who will provide most of the actual services. It is important to remember that each of these target groups for each program will receive an individualized group of marketing strategies.

Chapter 6

Positioning the Health Organization into the Minds of the Health Consumers and Providers

POSITIONING STATEMENTS

One of the most important aspects of marketing planning for a health care service is the use of market positioning. Before you begin to develop specific marketing strategies and tactics for select segments and targets, the health organization must consider the positioning or market niches it desires to obtain. MARKET POSITIONING is an attempt to distinguish the health care organization from its competitors along real dimensions in order to be the preferred service to select segments of the marketplace. Positioning aims to educate the medical provider and consumer along real differences between alternative services. This differentiation assists providers and consumers in matching themselves to the service that can be of most value. The tool of positioning is 1) image-making, 2) perception-oriented, and 3) personality-directed. The organization develops an image, perception, and a personality in the minds of the consumer.

Positioning is not necessarily a new tool in marketing. Historically, the concept of positioning was mainly concerned with what marketers did to the service or product being marketed. Today, it usually relates to what the health administrator or marketer does for the service in the minds of the provider or consumer. The original aspect of positioning was derived from "product positioning" which utilized the product's physical appearance, size, form, and price compared to its competitors. Today, it is important to market the organization's image, but it is vital to create a position in the provider's or consumer's mind. The following questions need to be answered to lay the framework for the development of a positioning strategy for the health care service:

1. How is my service currently perceived by the marketplace?
2. What do I want my providers/consumers to think of my service?
3. What are the weaknesses and strengths of my services?
4. Have I emphasized the service's strengths and can I improve the weaknesses?
5. What are the strengths and weaknesses of my competitors?
6. What is the "positioning gap" that is apparent in my competitors' services and how can I fill the gap?
7. How can I influence the prospective or existing provider/consumer to perceive my services related to the market position I desire?

All of these questions lay the framework for the development of a POSITIONING STRATEGY. The positioning strategy describes what your service stands for, how you would like providers/consumers to think of your services, and how you will communicate the positioning perception of the service to your providers/consumers in the community. Today's health care marketplace is no longer responsive to the strategies that worked in the past. There are just too many products, services, programs, and facilities. In this overcommunicated marketplace there is a strong need to be selective and concentrate on specific target groups and communicate to these groups using narrowly defined strategies. One of these key strategies is the POSITIONING of your programs or services into the mind of the medical provider or health consumer.

APPLICATION OF POSITIONING
TO LONG-TERM CARE SERVICES

The proliferation of new services and increased demand for their services has required long-term and senior care administrators to "position" their services in the minds of consumers. Marketers in all sectors of the health industry will be trying to communicate to the senior sector of the population during the next decade.

The maturing of the American population has brought about a more highly educated and discriminating consumer for senior care services. It has also created a tremendous current and future demand for these services. "Smart positioning" will have to replace "hard positioning" in marketing to the mature population and their families. It will become very difficult to con the senior marketplace as the educational levels of this group become higher and higher. Proven services with quality dimensions and positions in the marketplace will be the successful ones since this expanding group is quality-oriented. Products/services have to be marketed using more detailed information about the services. Proven services and word of mouth recommendations will be selected. Peer group pressure to try something new just because it is new or innovative will not be as effective.

The maturity market comprises at least 44 million individuals and one-third of all households. This group is quality-oriented and demands long-lasting effects from services. It will be a major mistake to market to the senior marketplace the same as the youth market. It demands a different positioning strategy. These strategies must relate to the senior marketplace in terms of quality, proven worthiness, and long-lasting qualities of the products or service.

One of the basic methods for developing positioning strategies is to apply them to the components of the marketing mix. In other words, positioning strategies can be developed according to the marketing mix components of pricing, place, product, and promotion.

The following are some examples of specific market positioning strategies, as applied to long-term or senior care services:

PRICING THE LONG-TERM CARE SERVICE can be a powerful positioning strategy in order to attract an adequate market share without also attracting a devastating competitive reaction. For example, some pricing strategies could be related to developing perceptions within the community:

1. Are the prices of the services to be perceived as "high-priced and high-quality" or as "low-priced and quantity-oriented" for easier access to care?
2. Depending upon the local reimbursement levels, are the services to be priced at a level related to Medicare coverage or will there be a higher co-payment?

The medical provider who refers clients to your services or the consumer who directly seeks care will develop an image or perception within their minds about how your services are priced. In other words, think how you would like the community to perceive your services' costs and fees.

THE CHARACTERISTICS OF THE SERVICE are a way to differentiate one's services by positioning the service to be general or specialized, available to all mature adults or to select segments of the marketplace, provided in a personal or factory-line mode of delivery, or by a courteous or disrespectful staff. The product component of the marketing mix relates to the physical aspects of the service or the way in which it is delivered. The following are some other examples of positioning questions:

1. Do medical providers and discharge planners perceive the senior service as highly professional and easy to work with or as difficult and unprofessional?
2. Does my staff perceive our organization as possessing a good physical environment in which to work?

All quality of care, staff relations, procedures, cleanliness, and service are involved in positioning the service through the use of the product component of the marketing mix.

THE WAY IN WHICH SERVICES ARE DELIVERED is important in relationship to the services being perceived as highly accessible or limited in accessibility, flexible in hours, possessing adequate parking and public transportation, operating in a safe location, or requiring a short waiting period before service is rendered.

The place component is a very important one as it relates to location, mode of delivery, and access to care. These three characteristics can be very important to the senior care client.

HOW ONE PROMOTES THEIR SERVICES positions the service as being hard sell, soft sell, educational, or good will-oriented; serving the community or just the financial needs of the organization; or being widely or little known within the community.

Other examples would be the questions:

1. Is the organization perceived as being secretive or readily available to distribute needed information about the services or treatment procedures?
2. Does the community perceive our service as being professional if we advertise on the radio or in the newspaper?

All of these positioning strategies relate to the amounts, quality, and direction of the information communicated to the population.

Since advertising is becoming much more common in health care it is important to be selective of the media channel. Populations perceive an organization's position according to which media channel is utilized.

BEING FIRST INTO THE MARKETPLACE

In an overcommunicated marketplace positioning becomes an organized system for entering the consumer's mind. The easiest way in which to make a mental impression is to be first into the marketplace. The organization can build loyalty for the services by getting there first and providing no reason for the health consumer to ever switch. History demonstrates that the first product or service into the consumer's mind gets twice the long-term market share as that of the nearest competitor. The major reason that market leaders lose market share is change.

An example of being first for a positioning strategy is the new expansion of Life Care Services. Life Care is still a relatively new concept integrating the traditional services of a retirement community with the long-term health care found in a nursing home. There are some 600 Life Care Communities throughout the United States. The services for residents include: medical care, transportation, living quarters, personal assistance, emergency service, funeral expenses, recreational activities, counseling, and continuing education centers. With the population maturing at such a fast pace, these initial Life Care Communities may have positioned themselves successfully for the long-term.

REPOSITIONING IN A HIGHLY COMPETITIVE ENVIRONMENT

The majority of the time most services cannot be the first into a marketplace. Most health services, especially senior services, are in the maturity phase of their existence and have many competitors. The traditional positioning strategy is to reposition the organization in the minds of the consumer. It is necessary to move the positioning of the competitors out of the minds of the consumer. This can be accomplished by positioning the services as being better or providing a key service which the competition does not. Comparative positioning is not illegal in most cases. Performed honestly, comparative repositioning can be positive for the marketplace. It keeps the providers alert and responsive to the needs of the community. Health care organizations have used repositioning extensively as related to offering services in a unique fashion or emphasizing better quality of care than its competitors.

COMPETING DIRECTLY WITH YOUR COMPETITORS

Most organizations do not attempt to take on the strongest competitor in the marketplace. You can go around, under, or over, but never directly against the dominant provider. The position required in this case is to take advantage of weaknesses or gaps in the marketplace. A great example of this positioning strategy is the HMO marketplace in Northern California where Kaiser's HMO is the dominant force. Yet over twelve new HMOs have been developed during the last decade. These new HMOs market themselves related to services not available through Kaiser, better fees, etc. The new HMOs identified a niche in the marketplace and went after it. These new HMOs are trying to position themselves as being differentiated from Kaiser in terms of weaknesses in the Kaiser system or gaps in service delivery within the marketplace.

POSITIONING WITH A GOOD NAME

Goodwill and brand loyalty are vitally important concepts in marketing health care organizations. People want to be "attached" to a particular health care organization or service for security and trust factors. One of the most important aspects of brand loyalty is developing a quality and memorable name for the organization. Health care organizations have traditionally been delinquent in deciding on marketing-related names for their services.

Developing a name for a service can be approached from various perspectives. First of all, a strong positioning name is one in which the consumer relates to the type of service provided. For example, the Meals on Wheels program reflects a uniqueness and explains the basic service which is provided. A second approach is to keep the name simple yet find a unique marketing niche for the name. For example, a local crisis telephone line having the name Talk Line with the actual phone number related to the letters in the name is well-positioned. A third perspective is to be creative and develop a catchy name with a historical perspective, such as On Lok Senior Health Services. Other senior services with well-positioned names include: Gray Panthers, Senior Escort, Retirement Jobs, Inc., Golden Gate Senior Service, and YMCA Christmas Camp for Seniors. Sometimes a full name is not necessary as abbreviations become the positioning strategy. Think about the recognition and positioning of names such as: HHS, L-T-C, HUD, IBM, CARE, WHO, UN, AMA, and AHA. These are powerful positioning statements and highly recognizable.

POSITIONING SLOGANS AND LOGOS

An increasing concept in thinking about positioning the service is the use of slogans which represent these services. A slogan usually represents 1) a feeling we want to express about our services and 2) a key characteristic of the service. Slogans can be very creative and stylish. Who can forget "Where's the Beef?", "I Ate the Whole Thing!", "It Takes Two Hands to Handle a Whopper!", "Ring Around the Collar!", "Reach Out and Touch Someone," or "We Try Harder!"? These products were successfully positioned in the minds of the consumer by these slogans. Some examples in health care include a dental service named Smile America and its slogan "Smile America is here to keep you smiling." The slogan reflects the purpose of the preventive cleaning service and is also memorable. Another example would be a wellness program with its slogan "Let's Work Together for Life." A third example would be St. Luke's Hospital of Kansas City's "100—A Century of Service/A Heritage of Excellence."

An alternative to a slogan can be a well-developed logo for the organization. There are successful organizations which just specialize in developing the most appropriate and potentially effective logo for a specific organization. A well-developed logo can position the service in the minds of the consumer. One of the most successful logos and symbols in health care is the picture of the palms of two hands with a rainbow underneath representing United Way. Another successful one has been the Family Service Agency's symbol of two adults and two children within an oval parameter. Others include Blue Shield's medical insignia involving the staff of Aesculapius; Blue Cross' cross with an artist's sketch of a person in the middle with a circle around him; The Blood Center for Southwest Louisiana's two hearts on top of each other with one heart filled with blood dripping into the bottom of the heart; Adventist Health System-West's map of the United States marked off with the western states for territory they serve; and many different wellness programs with their derivative of a rising sun logo.

SUMMARY OF POSITIONING

Positioning can be one of the most powerful and long-lasting marketing tools. It is an integral part of any strategic marketing plan. The positioning section of the plan should include a laundry list and qualitative discussion of the specific positions which the organization desires to imprint into the minds of its consumers and providers. Positioning services requires some creativity, risk-taking, vision for the future, adaptability to change, subtleness, patience, and a willingness to use marketing as a key tool. Before any marketing strategies are developed in our next steps, positioning statements and thoughts must be analyzed and agreed upon by the marketing committee. These images and perceptions direct us to develop specifically applied strategies which will inform us how to position these services in the minds of the consumer.

SUMMARY FOR CHAPTER 6:
POSITIONING THE HEALTH ORGANIZATION
INTO THE MINDS OF THE
CONSUMERS AND PROVIDERS

Before creating marketing strategies and tactics, it is important to examine what perceptions our target groups already have about the organization and to decide on specific perceptions we desire to have these groups possess. There are many ways to examine the use of positioning. The reader should have developed an understanding of: 1) the basic concepts of market positioning; 2) applications of positioning to the components of pricing, product, place, and promotion; being first into the marketplace; establishing positioning oriented names and slogans, etc.; and 3) how positioning lays the framework along with the marketing missions, goals, objectives, auditing, and targeting for developing marketing strategies and tactics.

Market positioning is a form of market strategy development. All of the actions we select to market the services to the target groups must be directed toward achieving select market positions.

This chapter lays the framework for the next one which thoroughly examines the creative phase of marketing—the development of strategies and tactics.

CASE EXAMPLE:
MARKET POSITIONING OF A PREVENTIVE
DENTAL CARE CENTER

INTRODUCTION

This short case is presented to demonstrate the applicability of the positioning techniques discussed in the prior chapter. The emphasis is a need to differentiate the health and human service from its competitors in the minds of the consumer. In this case, the reader is shown the positioning niches in the marketplace for a preventive dental service. The dental service is attempting to distinguish itself from other similar or identical dental practices according to unique characteristics of the practice.

BACKGROUND

A private dental group practice owned by Dr. Smith Johnson opened up PreventCare in the downtown financial district of the San Diego, CA metropolitan area. Dr. Johnson was in partnership with three other practicing dentists. The dentists also maintain two conventional dental practices in the same geographic area. Dr. Johnson and his partners had been in general dentistry in the San Diego area for approximately ten years. As more and more local dental graduates started practices or were attracted from other locales to this desirable region of the country, the level of competition began to increase significantly. They began to experience a stagnation of demand for their services from new patients. This situation stimulated them to investigate new market opportunities. Dr. Johnson commissioned a marketing consultant to evaluate the dental market in the San Diego area. The results of the market analysis indicated a large gap in traditional dental services in the downtown area of the City. Dr. Johnson then contracted with the same marketing consultant to explore the need for preventive-type dental services. The consultant surveyed a sample of employee benefit directors in local corporations, small business owners, random street interviews, and hotel/restaurants within a two-mile radius of the center of the downtown financial district. The questionnaire attempted to inquire as to their use of preventive dental services, and if used, to question the need for such a new service in the area. The survey identified a demand for such services but some confusion as to what preventive dental services were and how busy white collar workers would be able to obtain them during working hours. The consultant then identified that there was not only no such type of service in this area, but no dental practices in the country which totally dedicated themselves to preventive services for this group of workers. Dr. Johnson discussed these findings with his partners and financial planner. Dr. Johnson and his partners began to firmly believe there was a market for a preventive dentistry-type service. They decided to open a small store front preventive dental service in a busy section in the middle of the downtown financial district of San Diego. The name they decided upon was PreventCare. (It should be noted that three major positioning decisions have already been made by the dentists: type of service, location, and name. First of all, there is no similar service in the area; only preventive services will be provided; and the name PreventCare is simple to remember and reflects the purpose for their existence and the service rendered.)

PREVENTCARE SERVICES

PreventCare offers cleaning, brushing, polishing, and preventive check-ups with x-rays on a walk-in or appointment basis. It is open five days per week from 7 am to 6 pm. A licensed dentist is available at all times with a dental hygienist and a receptionist. It is attractively decorated with hanging plants, comfortable sofas and chairs, and a snack tray and wine. All prices are approximately 20% lower than the average private dental practice.

TARGET GROUPS

From the marketing analysis the consultant identified the following groups as the most promising primary and secondary marketing targets to pursue:

1. Young, upwardly mobile white collar workers in the downtown area; these workers were limited to ages 18-45, working within a five-block radius of the practice;

2. Since San Diego is a major tourist attraction, tourists became a possible walk-in target group;
3. Conventioneers from the nearby convention center and many local hotels;
4. Shoppers from the five main downtown shopping malls;
5. Students from three nearby colleges;
6. Restaurateurs from the local 130 restaurants; and
7. Construction workers from the ten high rise projects being completed in the downtown area.

POSITIONING PREVENTCARE

As part of the marketing strategies for PreventCare, the positioning aspects became important in order to make a strong mental impression upon the potential target groups and to develop service loyalty. The unique characteristics which will cause these target groups to potentially use PreventCare reflect the organization's position in the marketplace and in the minds of the consumers.

Positioning Statement or Slogan

The positioning statement became "Come to PreventCare and leave with a better smile within twenty minutes!" This statement related to the characteristics of the service (cleaning), walk-in availability (no appointments), quick service (20 minutes or less), and physical improvement (improved smile). These basic ingredients comprised the framework for the positioning strategies.

Positioning Characteristics of the Service

The most important aspect of positioning is to have all aspects of the service reflect the image of the positioning statement. The unique characteristics, or positions, of PreventCare were developed to create client perceptions according to the following:

— Quick service—i.e., come in during your lunch hour, before work, after work, or by appointment;
— Convenience with no appointments necessary—i.e., walk-in service at any time;
— Geared toward self-gratification and appearance of upwardly mobile and ambitious people;

— Pleasant environment—i.e., plants, wine, comfortable furniture, boutique-oriented, modern pictures on walls, classical music, up-to-date modern literature on tables, glass partitions, handsomely dressed and very pleasant receptionist, etc.;
— Reasonable costs—i.e., large display and brochures listing exact prices for services;
— Back-up of full dentistry office—i.e., two offices within walking distance if needed;
— Emphasis on prevention—i.e., cleaning prevents future problems;
— Creative and modern quality service—i.e., relating to young, upwardly mobile people;
— Personal decision—i.e., emphasis on placing the responsibility on these young adults to decide when, and if, their teeth need cleaning rather than the dentist telling them so;
— Quality service with professionally trained and experienced dentists and hygienists to serve you.

All of the brochures, flyers, advertisements, and other information pieces constantly projected the positioning perceptions of these characteristics in the minds of the target groups selected in the marketing plan. The next step for the dental practice is to develop specific marketing actions (strategies and tactics) which will reflect these positioning characteristics and will be used to attract new patients. It is important to remember that all of the positioning characteristics can be transformed into strategies and tactics.

Chapter 7

Developing Marketing Strategies and Tactics

STRATEGY FORMULATION PROCESS

After identifying segments and targets to whom to direct the marketing activities, the action phase begins in the planning process. As the reader can tell no actual marketing activities have taken place to communicate to the organization's publics. This is a very important concept to understand in marketing. No action is taken before all of the prior steps have been completed as background. One of the major reasons for programs failing is the common error of jumping the gun and initiating strategies and tactics before solidly completing the prior marketing planning functions.

To better understand the step we are about to undertake, a schematic diagram of the strategy development process is demonstrated below:

[Marketing Missions, Goals, and Objectives]
↓
[Marketing Audit: Economic/Demographic/Technical/Etc.]
↓

Market Analysis	Industry Analysis	Competitor Analysis	Resource Analysis	Supplier Analysis

↓
[Segmentation and Targeting]
↓
[Positioning Analysis]
↓
[Desirable Marketing Strategies and Tactics]
↓
[Workable Strategies and Tactics]

This schematic diagram demonstrates the interrelationship of the systematic approach that is necessary for strategic marketing planning. Marketing strategies and tactics will be developed as an outcome of the prior steps in the planning process. In other words, the strategies and tactics must:

1. be consistent with the original marketing mission;
2. attempt to satisfy specific goals and objectives;
3. be directed to select target groups which are based on the audit analysis; and
4. be in sync with the positioning niche which the organization desires to possess in the marketplace.

WHAT ARE MARKETING STRATEGIES AND TACTICS?

MARKETING STRATEGIES outline a broad plan of action to best use the organization's health resources to achieve a marketing goal and objective. In addition, marketing strategies are the specific actions taken by the organization to communicate with the select primary target groups. MARKETING TACTICS are specific plans of action which further define specific marketing strategies. The interrelationship between strategies and tactics is similar to the differentiation described between marketing goals and objectives in Chapter 3. In other words, objectives further describe goals just as tactics additionally define strategies. Several samples of strategies and tactics will be provided but a basic example would be the following for marketing a hospital's wellness program to the target of commuters:

Marketing Strategy: to develop an advertising campaign for the hospital.

Marketing Tactic: to run an ad for the wellness clinic at the hospital on the local radio station.

In this example the marketing strategy briefly describes the action to be taken in marketing the hospital's wellness clinic. The marketing tactic describes the strategy in greater detail with specific information. There can even be MARKETING SUB-TACTICS which can describe the marketing tactic. For the example above, more information about the radio ad may be available. Therefore, a sub-tactic could be created such as: to advertise on the radio station with three one-minute ads; during the morning commute period; and spread out one per hour during the three hour commute program. In addition, for every marketing strategy there are typically multiple marketing tactics developed. *As a guideline for a typical marketing plan should be the presence of three to four marketing strategies for each target group and two to three marketing tactics for each marketing strategy.*

FRAMEWORK FOR DEVELOPING THE FIVE MOST COMMON MARKETING STRATEGIES

In today's competitive environment health organizations are exploring some very common, broad marketing strategies. These are MARKET PENETRATION, VERTICAL INTEGRATION, HORIZONTAL INTEGRATION, NEW SERVICE DEVELOPMENT, and DIVERSIFICATION. It is important to briefly differentiate these basic strategies because of their implementation by the majority of health organizations. These strategies are differentiated according to their application to the typical community hospital.

MARKET PENETRATION: This is the action of obtaining more patients for the present hospital and its current services. It is a typical strategy implemented to sustain or increase the hospital's market share of its current target groups. Currently many hospitals just want to communicate more effectively to the service area they have always served and to attract more of this existing group to use their hospital over another hospital.

MARKET EXPANSION: This is the action of attracting patients from new target groups and marketplaces. The difference with this strategy is to market to entirely new segments for an increase in the utilization of existing services. For example, many hospitals are attempting to attract segments of the community to use the hospital that live in areas geographically located outside of their usual service area.

VERTICAL INTEGRATION: This strategy is related to attracting more patients by adding to the supply side of existing services. In other words, vertical integration implies, for example, taking over similar hospitals in the community by takeover, merger, or a sharing process. The hospital is still in the hospital business and it is still providing similar services to what it used to offer except for an increase in the amount of these services. The proprietary hospital chains are a great example of vertical integration through the years as these firms have added similar hospitals through purchase, construction, or management contracts.

HORIZONTAL INTEGRATION: This action differentiates from horizontal integration by the addition of new services to the hospital's offering. The hospital is still in the hospital business—it has not added any new entire hospitals to its organizational structure—but it has attempted to increase the number of patients by attracting them to utilize entirely new services not previously offered. This is reflective of hospitals expanding into wellness programs, same-day surgery centers, urgent care centers, pharmacies, and laboratories during recent years.

DIVERSIFICATION: This action is usually mistaken for either vertical or horizontal integration. The marketing definition of diversification implies adding programs or purchasing other organizations that offer services which your organization never offered. These services are typically out of the usual scope of the hospital's business line. For example, hospitals are currently diversifying out of the hospital industry into real estate, consulting, investment banking, and in some cases, retail activities. This diversification is occurring as liquidity, profit margins, and return on investments shrink due to reimbursement constraints.

One or more of these broad marketing strategies is at the base of most hospital marketing campaigns in this country.

DEVELOPING MARKETING STRATEGIES BASED ON THE SERVICE LIFE CYCLE

Regardless of service type, geography, or marketplace, certain broad strategies seem to be appropriate based only on the STAGE OF THE SERVICE IN ITS LIFE CYCLE. As mentioned in the first chapter, every health organization "lives a life similar to human beings, meaning Introduction, Growth, Maturity, and Decline Phases." It is important for the administrator or marketer to identify the strength of its current service activity base and place it in its appropriate life cycle phase. Of course, there can be instances where an organization is on the borderline between two phases or experiencing characteristics of two different phases. However, typically the health organization settles into a distinct life cycle phase. This distinction allows for the development of individualized marketing strategies related to the select life cycle phase. The following characteristics and strategies are broadly applied to each phase. It is hoped that some of these basic characteristics can be helpful in developing unique strategies for the services.

INTRODUCTION PHASE: In the introduction phase the health organization's service is new to the marketplace. The common characteristics for services in this life cycle are:

a) There is a consumer group unaware of the service offered;

b) A limited number of varieties of the basic service are usually offered by the organization;

c) Emphasis is placed on market penetration and encouragement for consumers to "trial use" the service;

d) Concentration on the most interested and promising target group is initiated;

e) A positioning statement of quality service is the main framework;

f) Service probably faces future competition and it is preferable to build brand preference and loyalty by the most promising target groups;

g) A monitoring system is established to tract customer usage patterns and perceptions; and

h) Pricing and promotion can be directed in different ways for achieving the desired market penetration. These different pricing and promotion strategies can be grouped into:

RAPID-SKIMMING: setting a high price and having high levels of promotion to rapidly enter the market for those who can pay the high price. The promotion tends to justify the high price and relates the price to a quality service.

SLOW-SKIMMING: having a high price but low promotion. This is directed to keeping marketing expenditures low, enlarging the profit margin, not facing stiff future competition, having a consumer group aware of the service, and directing our attention to those targets which can afford the high price. Rapid-skimming strategies desire to penetrate the market quickly and hang on to their share of the market for a long time through service loyalty and referrals. The slow-skimming strategy is differentiated by no future competition and an emphasis on penetrating the market and building service loyalty over a long time frame. For example, open-heart procedures were good examples of rapid-skimming when many hospitals got on the bandwagon and charged extremely high charges for these sophisticated techniques and promoted their availability at the facility extensively. In comparison, plastic surgery techniques in the 1960s and early 1970s were very high priced but promoted sparingly (slow-skimming). These services were directed at a select high income group and the organizations and providers of these services were willing to build service loyalty very slowly.

RAPID PENETRATION: strategies in the introduction phase are related to charging a low price with high promotion. This mix of pricing and promotion encourages rapid acceptance by a wider number of segments in the marketplace. The strategy attempts to go after a large share of the market quickly. The market for these services is generally large and is aware of the services rendered. The consumers are price sensitive and there is usually strong competition for similar services currently or in the near future. For example, hospitals expanded their outpatient departments during this last decade. These services attempted to position themselves into the minds of the consumer as being lower-priced than traditional inpatient services and were heavily promoted to the many segments in the community.

SLOW PENETRATION: implies a low pricing policy with low amounts of promotion. This strategy encourages rapid acceptance of the service by the marketplace, keeps marketing costs low, markets to a large number of segments, has a service which is very price sensitive for consumers, possesses little or no competition, and has a consumer base which is not motivated very much by promotion programs. An example of this type of service which utilizes a slow penetration strategy is public health programs. Typically, public health programs, especially educational services, have been terribly marketed through the years. However they have used this type of strategy by possessing a very low price (free in many cases); having little money to promote to the general public; desiring rapid penetration by a large marketplace of all income levels; and having almost no competition for similar services.

The second major phase of a service's life cycle is the GROWTH PHASE. In this phase services are characterized by:

a) Experiencing its fastest sales or utilization trend;
b) Selecting the most profitable delivery mode;
c) A drop in price if competition materializes;
d) A constant planning for targets to add for future utilization;

e) Making sure services are available for consumers when they desire them;

f) Developing alternatives or options of the original service for maximum utilization;

g) Beginning to design a potential successor service;

h) Reinvesting some cash flow from the service to maximize efficiency of service delivery; and

i) Promotion and pricing strategies are dependent upon market conditions. Typically this phase is characterized by a strong word of mouth or referral process. The service is constantly being improved and we are adding other services to substitute or compliment the main service. New competitors are also present in order to cash in on your main service's success. Demand is still increasing at an increasing rate while the price for the service remains the same or begins to fall. The marketer usually decides the right time during this phase to lower prices to attract the next layer of price sensitive consumers. We tend to start searching for new segments or new delivery modes in the marketplace in order to keep this exponential growth continuing. At this point in time consumers are well aware of the service so promotion shifts toward service acceptance and actual purchase instead of education about the need for the service. In many ways the health organization must face the trade-off between emphasizing the strategies for obtaining a higher market share versus earning a higher profit margin. Examples of services which have experienced these characteristics during growth periods have been: family counseling, hospice centers, home care programs, and preferred provider organizations. In other words, every service will experience a growth phase with various degrees of these characteristics. However, the majority of services are usually faced with strategies related to 1) attempting to continue the growth phase; 2) positioning the service in the minds of the consumer against strong competition; 3) using pricing and promotion more effectively; and 4) developing alternative services to complement or potentially substitute the original service.

The third phase every service typically experiences is the MATURITY PHASE. *Most health and human services in the United States are currently in the mature phase of their life cycle.* Therefore, this phase may be the most important to many hospital, clinic, public health, and long-term care administrators. During this phase demand starts to slow down and the health organization may be characterized by being in this phase longer than any other. For example, most older community hospitals are definitely mature services and have been for a considerable amount of time. So, most marketing strategies deal with the mature phase in our health industry.

There are usually considered three main sub-phases of maturity for the health service: CONTINUED GROWTH MATURITY, STAGNANT MATURITY, and DECAYING MATURITY. Continued growth maturity is a sub-phase in which the services start to experience increasing demand but at a decreasing rate. In other words, the market is still expanding but the marginal increases are smaller and market saturation is materializing. Stagnant maturity is a second sub-phase in which demand levels off due to definite market saturation. Most growth during this sub-phase is occurring due to replacement and population growth rather than pure attraction to the main service. The decay maturity sub-phase experiences a definite gradual decline in demand as consumers begin to move toward other competitor services. This sub-phase possesses very apparent intense competition and a marketplace which is overcrowded. The three main strategies used for services or products which are in one of the maturity sub-phases are: MODIFICATION OF THE SERVICE'S MARKETPLACE, MODIFICATION OF THE SERVICE; and MODIFICATION OF THE MARKETING-MIX.

Modifying the service's marketplace involves finding new consumers, markets, target groups, and stimulating greater utilization by current clients for the existing service. Repositioning the service in the minds of new segments which haven't been addressed before can be a very successful strategy. For example, an HMO could have been mainly attracting the middle-income, union members and their families. There are many additional segments such as younger, poorer, and older groups which have not been served.

Modifying the actual service involves changing "real" characteristics of the service. This can be a physical and quality-related change. A new feature to the service can be added. In addition, the strategy is aimed at improving the style of the service (in other words, changing the positioning of the aesthetic appeal of the service rather than the functional attractions). A great example of services implementing this type of change are group practices of various types of medical providers. Tremendous competition has materialized for the typical community physician group practice in urban areas. This has led, for example, to groups opening their offices on weekends and even reinstituting home visits by the medical provider!

Modifying the market-mix implies changing the four Ps of marketing: pricing, place, product, and promotion. *These four Ps do not operate independently.* They must be *orchestrated* together for a successful marketing strategy. Therefore, for example, our same group practice in the prior paragraph could decide to develop a sliding fee schedule for office visits (PRICE); expand their office hours in the evening (PLACE); add on some new specialties to the practice (PRODUCT); and begin to distribute higher quality and more informative brochures about the changes in the other marketing mix components to the community (PROMOTION).

In summary, the maturity phase is characterized by:

a) Keeping constant changes in existing services to a minimum;

b) Concentrating on select market segments;

c) Expanding the life cycle through service redesign for new potential segments in the marketplace;

d) Increasing client follow-up or complimentary services; and

e) Arranging for promotion to restimulate demand for the service.

The final phase of the life cycle for a service is the DECLINE PHASE. In this phase the demand for the service is rapidly or slowly declining due to technological changes, new substitutes in the marketplace, or changes in client tastes for the service. Typically, health services in this phase can hang on for a considerable amount of time or be discontinued quickly. In many cases, services can last forever if the service is a main part of the organization's mission and philosophy. For example, many clinics directed toward lower income clients and associated with religiously affiliated hospitals are definitely in the decline phase. Some of these clinics have been in decline for many years but the service represents the backbone mission of the religiously oriented hospital in serving poor patients. Unfortunately, economic changes in Medicaid and Medicare reimbursement are beginning to force some of these clinics to be discontinued. The strategies typically used in this phase are: a decision to drop the service and reallocate resources to more cost-effective investments, reduce expenses as much as possible, concentrate current resources in the strongest segments, or develop compliment services which receive higher reimbursement in order to counter the decline aspects of the main service. During very recent years the old-fashioned in-patient revenue base is beginning to experience a decline phase in many community hospitals around the country. However, these services will still represent the main focus of the community hospital. Alternative services are being emphasized in order to counter any revenue decline.

Most of these life cycle strategies are broad and should not be taken as definitive rules. In addition, the length of any one phase can vary dramatically for different services. However, since health administrators and marketers must preserve revenue generator services, knowing the characteristics of strategies related to the life cycle can be helpful. One common point is the fact that most services maximize their cash flow to the organization at the end of the growth phase and during maturity. Therefore, strategies related to extending the growth and maturity phases may justify priority. The strategies related to this important cash flow period are related to: redesigning the actual service for new segments; adding complements to the main service, such as follow-up care; refining the components of the marketing mix so they are orchestrated; implementing a cost control mechanism into the marketing function; and beginning developing future substitute services.

SPECIFIC EXAMPLES OF MARKETING STRATEGIES

The foundation of strategies must be directed to concentrating on what must be done, where it must be done, and when it must be done to communicate with select targets and satisfy specific goals and objectives. Strategies can be developed in many different ways. One additional method is to develop strategies as applied to the components of the marketing mix. It is important to always fall back on the marketing mix for developing marketing strategies. The following lists examples of actual marketing strategies and tactics for a typical hospital, as applied to each component of the marketing mix.

The assumed marketing goal will be: TO INCREASE IN-PATIENT UTILIZATION.

The assumed marketing objective related to this goal will be: TO INCREASE PATIENT UTILIZATION BY 10% BEFORE DECEMBER.

The target groups will be: GENERAL PUBLIC OR PHYSICIANS.

Price Strategies:

1. Establish quantity discounts to encourage larger unit purchases of the services.
Tactics: a) Give percentage discounts for families who use the OB units of the hospital for their second, third, etc. child. b) For patients using outpatient pharmacy services, offer discounts to extended users.

2. Expand the use of credit for patients with large deductibles or co-payments.
Tactics: a) Expand the use of credit cards for patients. b) Offer hospital-backed loans for patients with catastrophic illnesses.

Place Strategies:

1. Develop a stronger relationship with attending physicians through construction.
Tactics: a) Build a professional medical building nearby to link physicians to the hospital. b) Offer the office space as a part-time second office to remote physicians.

2. Provide additional outlets for provision of services.
Tactics: a) Expand the use of the emergency room as a potential admitter for inpatients. b) Expand the hours the outpatient clinic is opened.

Product Strategies:

1. Distinguish the hospital's services from that of its competitors as viewed by your clients.
Tactics: a) Attract top medical providers in the community to become affiliated with the hospital. b) Develop an internal marketing program to make sure the hospital's staff believes and communicates the high quality of the services provided by the hospital.

2. Add new staff members who will become admitters.
Tactics: a) Assist physicians in relocating to existing offices attached to the hospital. b) Assist junior members of a group to establish their own private practices in the community.

Promotion Strategies:

1. Address advertising and promotion to key patients and best prospects.
Tactics: a) Have established medical staff give formal speeches at local business association meetings. b) Send brochures to employee benefit directors about the outpatient services available at the hospital.

2. Work with the city to improve hospital publicity.
Tactics: a) Construct additional signs to enhance hospital visibility on key access roads. b) Join the chamber of commerce so the hospital is listed for local businesses and general public.

These strategies and tactics are just examples of how a marketer or administrator can apply them to the components of the marketing mix. Additional examples of marketing strategies and tactics are described in the sample marketing plan in Chapter 9. One of the most important strategies that many organizations overlook is first developing an internal strategy base before marketing externally. The following section briefly describes the importance and examples of internal marketing strategies.

INTERNAL MARKETING STRATEGIES

Internal Marketing is the development of an organizational environment in which marketing becomes an integral part of our everyday managerial or clinical activities. In other words, a hospital, nursing home, or department must create a marketing orientation and philosophy for the entire organization and its employees. Marketing in health care organizations unfortunately begins by jumping the gun and initiating marketing strategies and tactics before most providers and staff understand their marketing roles within the organization. It is imperative to never market to the external community before internal marketing is completed.

All staff members in the health organization are using marketing with every interaction. Before initiating an internal marketing program it is important to relate to the patient as a client. Even with extensive insurance coverage most of the patients are involved in an exchange process with the health organization. The clients exchange money, time, inconvenience, and stress when obtaining typical health services. By relating to the patient as an exchange "client," it allows for a better acceptance of our role in marketing with every interaction.

Most internal marketing is related to 1) understanding that employees represent the health organization in marketing; 2) communicating effectively with our clients, providers, community representatives, or other employees; 3) providing for marketing oriented atmospherics; and 4) creating a long-run marketing philosophy for the entire organization.

All employees represent the organization for which they work. This is important because most of the clients develop their perceptions of the organization related to how they are treated while using the service. For example, their perceptions of the quality of care are typically determined by the way in which they interact with the employees of the health organization. If employees understand the importance of effective interaction, it can carry over to a referral being made by a satisfied client, employee, or provider. The major success of marketing health services is a satisfied client and receiving a referral. The quality of the interaction between an employee or provider and the client can be the key ingredient for this referral.

Some key suggestions in improving communication include:

1. Being careful to avoid highly technical jargon with a patient;
2. Listening carefully to the client;
3. Maintaining eye contact for establishing interest and trust;
4. Restating your ideas for clarity, especially when giving instructions to patients; and
5. Not being afraid to use appropriate body language and facial expressions when emphasizing certain points.

Other areas for effective internal marketing include: using the telephone effectively by greeting the caller, speaking distinctly, and not putting people on hold for long periods; being careful not to put people off by using typical sayings such as, "It's just routine," "This won't hurt," or "It's hospital policy"; remembering to smile; greeting people who look lost in our hospital complexes; introducing yourself; avoiding endearing names such as calling people "honey," "dear," or "darling"; trying to exceed people's expectations in giving information; complimenting a client when the opportunity arises; and presenting a professional image in terms of dress and physical presence.

The atmospherics, or physical environment, of the health organization also relate to internal marketing. Atmospherics include the physical layout, accessibility, waiting time for service, colors and furnishings, neatness of treatment area, smells or noises, and the efficiency of our treatment and triage systems. These environmental factors have an influence on the client's perception of the service being provided.

Nurses, medical providers, support staff, counselors, technicians, billing clerks, admission personnel, dietitians, and volunteers are some examples of the variety of people who come into contact with our clients. These people can better understand how they represent the organization through an effective internal marketing program. Making sure the organization is internally marketing-oriented can become the strategy which will lay the framework for successful external marketing endeavors.

An organization which is internally marketing-oriented provides a strong base from which to develop external marketing strategies. It also allows for more cost-effective marketing. This evaluation process is described in the next chapter through the use of a marketing control system.

SUMMARY FOR CHAPTER 7: DEVELOPING MARKETING STRATEGIES AND TACTICS

Most people associate marketing with public relations and advertising. These activities are included, finally, in the creative phase of marketing—strategy development.

This phase must include an entrepreneural spirit by the marketer and health organization. All of the prior steps in the planning process have finally led up to our "taking some action to communicate with the selected target groups." As the reader can tell, all of the prior steps have laid a base for strategy development. For example, the marketing missions, goals, and objectives direct us to specific purposes and outcomes we hope to achieve with the strategies that are implemented. The audit identified opportunities and assisted in selecting target groups to better direct to whom we are marketing. The positioning phase provided key niches in the marketplace the organization desires to possess and perceptions in the minds of the target groups that require nurturing.

The reader should have grasped an understanding of: 1) the strategy formulation process; 2) a framework for five very common market strategies being used today; 3) how to develop strategies for specific phases of the life cycle; 4) differentiation between market strategies and tactics; and 5) applications of strategy and tactic development to the components of the marketing mix.

This is the action phase of the strategic marketing plan. The success or failure of the plan will materialize from the measurement of the effectiveness of these strategies and tactics achieving the marketing missions, goals, and objectives established in the beginning planning steps. The next chapter discusses this evaluation or control process in addition to the important aspects of organizational design for marketing and the marketing budget process.

CASE EXAMPLE: MARKETING STRATEGIES AND TACTICS FOR TODAY'S MODERN COMMUNITY HOSPITAL WITHIN THE COMPLEX MEDICAL MARKETPLACE

The hospital industry is in a state of flux. There is a new look to hospital practice in most metropolitan and suburban areas of the country. The entrepreneural spirit is quite evident, and occasionally flamboyant in many of these areas. With occupancy rates on the decline for traditional inpatients and cost-cutting policies being initiated by government and private insurers, a marketing-oriented management style has emerged. This has become very important as hospital occupancy, for instance, has declined from a national average of 76% in 1980 to approximately 71% in 1984. Payments for inpatient care by third-party payors is under attack so hospitals are seeking new ventures to be developed. There is a whole new approach to health care as doctors and administrators begin to view themselves as highly trained businesspeople. The risk inherent in this change is that the contract between the health profession and society will be lost sight of as these changes progress. Just five years ago the idea that non-profit hospitals might actually think about and participate in competition with other hospitals would have been called a fantasy by many professionals, and a nightmare by others. Today, it is no longer the question of whether a hospital should compete, but it is a question of how to compete.

The question of how to compete is reflected in marketing strategy and tactic development within the marketing planning process.

Many of the changes in existing services and development of new services are part of the strategy formulation process. In response to the changing marketplace, hospitals around the country have developed some creative and entrepreneural strategies. Some of these include:

— Development of 365-day-a-year walk-in clinics;
— Acceptance of credit cards for payment;
— Expanded hours of most clinics;
— Additional services such as podiatrists, optometrists, chiropractors, and even acupuncturists;
— Advertising by mail, billboard, flyers, on transit, radio, TV, and newspapers;
— Development of same-day surgery centers;
— Development of home care programs;
— Renegotiated vendor contracts for cost-containment;
— Reduced staff for inpatient services or staff shifted to ambulatory centers;
— Established dietary consultation for other hospitals and nursing homes;
— Created "Meals On Wheels" programs for the elderly and handicapped;
— Contracted out the hospital's janitorial services to medical offices;
— Created urgent care centers, emergicenters, convenience care centers, etc.;
— Offers of bundle packages for physical exams, ob-gyn services, laboratory testing, etc.;
— Experimenting with cut-rate package offerings of hospital services or even complements such as gourmet meals and upper-income private rooms;
— Actually advertising prices for hospital services and even some comparative prices with other hospitals;
— Created sport care programs, wellness programs, etc.;
— Started risk reduction programs for executives and businesses for alcohol, drugs, stress, etc.;
— Created separate foundations as part of the hospital for fund raising or for-profit functions;
— Mass purchasing and shared services;
— Established consulting divisions for management consulting, employee benefit analysis for businesses, etc.;

— Transferred inpatient into outpatient services—i.e., brain scanning, health screening, laboratory testing, surgery, rehabilitation, etc.;
— Contracted with, or formed, PPOs, IPAs, HMOs, etc.

All of these strategies are quite creative for traditional hospitals. Of course, many investor-owned facilities have been experimenting with some of these ventures for some time. Hospitals in the nonprofit sector are getting a rude awakening to the realities of marketplace capitalism. The impacts of these changes, especially upon loss leader services being offered and access for the poor and elderly, are just now beginning to be examined. Installing competition does promote entrepreneural activity. Marketing strategy development is becoming one of the most important, and sought after, tools of marketers, planners, administrators, and board members.

Besides market strategies, it is important to remember that most public relations activities fall into the classification of market tactics. Tactics can vary dramatically in their scope but most of them are related to specific mechanisms for communicating with select target groups. For example, the following promotional tools, or tactics, are typically used in today's modern hospital:

* brochures * news releases * internal newsletters * external newsletters * public service announcements * factsheets * traveling displays * videotape presentations * educational forums * direct mail flyers * educational classes * social events * special business letters * seminars * symposiums * handbooks * manuals * bulletin boards * films * hotlines * information racks * speaker's bureaus * inserts * open houses * tours * news conferences * posters * public address systems * ~~nual reports * billboards * contests * signs, etc.

Chapter 8

Organizational, Budgeting, and Control Systems

CONTROL SYSTEMS

A control system is required to measure the performance and effectiveness of the marketing plan in achieving the plan's marketing goals and objectives. A control system is the step necessary to assure the plan is adjusted if necessary. Actual outcomes of the plan are measured against the original projected outcomes. Since every marketing plan will require some adjustment and refinement, it is important to remember that the marketing plan is not fixed. It has to be a flexible process which can be updated and altered when it is required. In addition, the planning process is never-ending so the control process must also be implemented periodically.

Control systems need to be an essential ingredient of the planning process. The feedback system:

1. Pinpoints problems and deviations;
2. Provides a mechanism for adjustment; and
3. Accumulates data for future planning.

The control or feedback system reflects the health organization's performance in obtaining its marketing objectives through the implementation of the strategic marketing plan. Since the goals and objectives are the comparison base it is important to make these goals and objectives as specific and measurable as possible. Some of these outcomes can be patient revenue, costs, profits, number of patients, utilization of services, changes in goodwill and image in the community, levels of quality of care, consumer preferences, etc. The control process is integrated into the planning process by the following flow:

PLANNING PROCESS ⟶ PLAN IMPLEMENTATION ⟶ PLAN RESULTS ⟶ EVALUATION OF RESULTS VERSUS GOALS AND OBJECTIVES ⟶ DECISIONS ON ALTERATIONS IN PLAN ⟶ PLANNING PROCESS.

The information flow is a key ingredient to a quality control system. The decision of which managers will receive what kinds and amounts of information in what time frames is the framework of a quality control process. A new planning cycle is initiated when these decisions and alterations have been completed. The base of a quality control system is the process of continuous reports back to managers reflecting the plan's performance level versus its goals and objectives.

The ingredients of a control system are:

1. Marketing goals and objectives;
2. Actual results of plan;
3. Projected results of plan;
4. Variance between actual and perceived outcomes; and
5. Decisions about changes in plan.

Performance should be evaluated on a monthly or on a bi-monthly basis. The plan should be evaluated frequently for alterations and identification of deviations. This evaluation process can be one of the most important steps in the entire planning process. It is the plan's only feedback system to boards, executives, and managers about the success of the strategic marketing plan. Therefore, an effective control system is required to measure performance, provide for effective action to correct deviations from expected standards, and communicate to management. Performance must be measured and analyzed as early as possible after implementation. When deviations are detected, their cause should be uncovered. Some questions which need to be asked when evaluating a plan's performance include:

1. Is utilization increasing at the expected rate?
2. Are referrals increasing?
3. Are the marketing goals and objectives realistic?
4. Is the marketing mix of pricing, place, product, and promotion correct?
5. Is additional marketing audit information needed?

6. Is enough money being spent on implementing the strategies?
7. Should we switch some of the primary and secondary targets?
8. Are marketing expenditures at levels planned?
9. Are the positioning strategies being imprinted in the minds of our consumers?
10. Should we evaluate (control) the outcomes of the plan more frequently?
11. Is our internal staff playing their roles in marketing the organization?
12. Should we switch some resources from one strategy to another which is being more effective?

Remember that the plan has not actually been implemented yet when the control system is being developed. This is the reason a control step is included in our strategic marketing plan. When the time comes for evaluating the performance of the plan, the marketer will be ready to implement the system.

MARKETING BUDGET

A projected marketing budget is an integral part of the marketing plan. The marketing budget reflects a projected total cost of developing, planning, and implementing the marketing program. The budget should include all direct and indirect expenses you expect to spend for successful completion of the strategic marketing plan. It needs to reflect, for example, a three-month development and planning process and a nine-month implementation process.

The typical types of expenses for a marketing program are:

I. MARKETING ADMINISTRATION SALARIES AND BENEFITS

A. Marketing Director
B. Public Relations Director
C. Marketing Research Assistant
D. Fund Raiser
E. Director of Planning
F. Administrative Assistant/Secretarial
G. Advertising Firm Fees
H. Public Relations Firm
I. Mail Order House

II. RENT AND UTILITIES

  A. Office Space
  B. Storage Space for Brochures and Supplies
  C. Telephone, Lights, etc.

III. OFFICE SUPPLIES

  A. Paper
  B. Equipment
  C. Word Processors

IV. TRAVEL

  A. Meeting Registration Fees
  B. Conventions
  C. Meals
  D. Hotels, Airfares, Car Rental

V. PROMOTIONAL EXPENSES

  A. Shows, Tours, Films, Open-Houses, Printing, Lectures, Seminars, Workshops, Posters, Mailers, Postage, Newsletters, Mail Order Houses, Brochures, Typesetting, Cocktail/Dinners, Signs, Newspaper Ads, Media Coverage, etc.

Marketing activities incur a considerable amount of expenses. For example, a decision might be made to mail out a brochure. The expenses involved include: designing the brochure, typesetting the brochure, printing the brochure, paper for brochure, stuffing by mail order houses, postage, envelopes, purchase of labels, labeling of envelopes, etc. As you can tell, each marketing activity has considerable costs which are not typically considered. Marketing can be very expensive when marketing research, advertising, and public relations firms are utilized. The projected budget needs to include as many expected and realistic expenditures as possible. One mistake is not to call for advice when developing an estimate. For example, very few people really know what it costs to rent time on a radio station or rent a billboard. Call the appropriate resources for accurate estimates.

A guideline for a total budget for marketing activities including marketing research, planning, fund development, and public relations can be about 1-3% of an organization's total annual budget. Most hospitals, for example, still spend less than 2% on these functions. In today's competitive marketplace, health organizations need to allocate a share closer to the high end of the scale for effectiveness. One of the key reasons for failure in marketing programs is the lack of financial support for the marketing function.

ORGANIZATIONAL DESIGN FOR MARKETING IN HEALTH ORGANIZATIONS

As part of the strategic marketing plan a design of the organizational chart for the marketing function is included. There are many different forms of organizational charts for marketing in health care organizations. This is especially true when some organizations' full-time directors of marketing, part-time directors, and others share the marketing function among all of their administrators. *Two important common ingredients in the organizational chart is the necessity of having the director of marketing report directly to the executive director and the functions of planning, public relations, fund raising, and marketing research report directly to the director of marketing.*

As an example, a proposed organizational chart for marketing in a large community hospital might look like the following. It is reflective of the organizational framework discussed in the first two chapters of text.

Board ------------ Board Marketing Committee

Executive Director --------- Legal Counsel

Vice President of Marketing ---- Organ. Marketing Committee
Director of Medical Staff
Director of Finance
Director of Planning
Director of Patient Care
Executive Director
Board Member From Board
Marketing Committee

Dir. of Marketing Research	Dir. of Fund Raising	Dir. of Public Relations	Dir. of Planning

THE MARKETING FUNCTION

The marketing director's role needs to include:

1. Setting up the marketing plan;
2. Directing the execution of the marketing plan; and
3. Evaluating and controlling the marketing plan.

The marketing director's position requires the ability and knowledge to do the following:

1. Know what the markets are;
2. Know where the markets are;
3. Know how to provide a quality health service;
4. Know how to provide the right service at the right time to the right target group at the right price;
5. Know how to be selective in targeting;
6. Possess an effective communications system including all four components of the marketing mix;
7. Continually strive to improve the service;
8. Continually strive to increase the marketshare;
9. Develop a strong relationship with internal staff and peers for marketing support; and
10. Develop a strong relationship with the board and executive director.

KEY TASKS OF THE DIRECTOR OF MARKETING

There are many different roles in which the marketing director must represent and perform. Most of these duties are typically found in informal job descriptions. They include being a(n):

1. EDUCATOR: The director of marketing will be continually educating its publics and staff about the importance, functions, and applications of marketing.

2. RESEARCHER: In order to understand the consumers he/she serves, the director of marketing needs to research consumer behavior, audit information, and competitor data.

3. PLANNER: By being in charge of the strategic planning process the marketer will need to be familiar with the different planning methodologies that are current in the field.

4. COORDINATOR: Coordinating and mobilizing marketing programs and resource allocation are a main function of the marketer.

5. LIAISON: The marketing director is a liaison with the community. The director represents the organization with all of the health service's publics. He/she also is the main lobbyist with special interest groups and legislative bodies.

6. MEDIA SPOKESPERSON: Many times the director represents the organization with the press and media, especially if a director of public relations or communications director does not exist.

7. MARKETING MANAGER: The director is in charge of multiple people and disciplines including research, planning, fund raising, board relations, etc. This requires excellent management abilities.

8. POLITICIAN: The marketing function requires tremendous internal political ability when dealing with power positions and territorial domains within the organization. The marketer is also the main lobbyist for the organization by interacting with government agencies and special interest groups.

9. FORECASTER: The marketer makes forecast of potential demand, utilization trends, resource requirements, and environmental changes.

10. COMMUNICATOR/PROMOTER: The marketer is a promoter for the organization. Charisma, personal energy, and ambition are important qualifications for the position. Excellent communication skills as well as technical marketing abilities are also important.

11. ADVISOR/CONSULTANT: Advising the executive director and board about potential changes or resource allocation decisions are part of the job. Giving advice is a key component of the position for members of the medical staff, regular management staff, etc.

12. CHANGE MASTER: The health environment is constantly changing. The marketing director must be able to identify these changes, recommend actions related to these changes, and be able to evaluate the potential impact on the organization of these changes. The marketer must anticipate, evaluate, and manage change.

The marketing function in the organization is not a vogue or a passing fad. The competition and reimbursement trends in the health field are real. Only those who have strong marketing talent on their management team will be able to survive in the coming years.

TRENDS IN SELECTION OF MARKETING DIRECTORS

It has been estimated by the American Marketing Association that over half of the hospitals in the United States will have a director of marketing by the late 1980s. This is a far cry from the less than 10% in 1980. Hospitals, HMOs, nursing homes, proprietary chains, home care agencies, same-day surgery centers, and other types of delivery mechanisms are seeking out professional assistance in marketing. Unfortunately, the early 1980s witnessed a trend for health organizations to attempt to make marketers out of planners, public relations directors, advertisers, community relations directors, and fund raisers. In fact, in most surveys three out of every four marketing directors possess no marketing background and they have been in their positions less than three years. In addition, the high expectations of what marketing will achieve and this lack of professional training in marketing has created a very high turnover rate of less than three years tenure in these positions.

The marketing directors in hospitals, for example, are coming from many different occupational and educational backgrounds. In fact, a very small percentage of today's marketing directors have had any service, industrial, or consumer goods experience. Either these professionals know the health industry well and are expected to learn marketing or they have strong marketing backgrounds with very little knowledge of the health industry. The directors are being derived from health insurance firms, industrial corporations, government agencies, health associations, consulting firms, consumer goods industries, HMOs, pharmaceutical and supply firms, and other sources. This trend is very typical in health care as there is a time lag between the demand for select backgrounds and the supply of qualified and trained personnel. Unfortunately, health administration education usually lags behind the needs of the marketplace. Speaking of education, it appears that most marketing directors have a graduate degree in health care administration, marketing, management, planning, social sciences, or physical sciences. This will shift toward a greater emphasis in health marketing and planning as the scope of the study advances as a specialty area in health administration education.

Health care marketing directors across the country are also still not equivalent in their functional areas to their counterparts in other industries. For example, most marketing directors in health care still are not organizationally settled with public relations, fund raising, community relations, marketing research, lobbying, and patient liaison activities reporting to this position. In many instances, the marketing function is on the same organizational level as these other areas. Probably the greatest area of activity for marketing directors still lies in planning, public relations, and promotion. One important area, physician and staff relations, appears to be negligible in most hospitals. In addition, the level of vice-presidency is not yet widespread for the marketing position. The titles of director, assistant administrator, planner, community relations director, and others prevail.

All of these characteristics of the state of the art of health marketing indicate that health marketing is becoming more accepted, understood, and utilized in health organizations. However, the learning process is slow while the demand for the service is high. It will be a decade before qualified marketing directors will be available for organizations seeking to fill well-defined marketing director positions. Organizations still have a considerable amount of learning to do about the need and overall application of marketing, while marketers require greater amounts of specific education in health care marketing and planning. When I was involved in developing one of the first graduate courses for practitioners in health care marketing over ten years ago I never envisioned such a spiraling interest in the scope of study and application. It is an exciting discipline which will continue to mature into an advanced management tool for health and human service administrators.

SUMMARY FOR CHAPTER 8: ORGANIZATIONAL, BUDGETING, AND CONTROL SYSTEMS

As the final step in the marketing plan, a thorough control system needs to be established to measure the effectiveness of the marketing plan. In other words, the control system answers the question, "How well did we meet the goals and objectives that were laid out in the beginning of the marketing plan?" This control system allows for the identification of any problems or deviations, and lays the groundwork for adjustments in the plan. No prior step in the plan should be considered fixed. Fine tuning of the plan is usually required for successful programs.

In addition, the marketing function in terms of organizational structure requires attention. Exactly who is going to be responsible for implementing and monitoring the marketing plan?

Of course, no marketing plan would be implemented without an accurate forecast of what it is going to cost. The budget process may be one of the most important areas to address when attempting to have administration or the board agree upon the implementation of the marketing plan.

The reader should have derived an understanding of: 1) the purpose, importance, and basic framework for a control system in the plan; 2) the role and tasks of a marketing director; and 3) the systematic process for creating a marketing budget.

This chapter completes the major steps that need to be included in a marketing plan. Chapter 10 provides an example of a condensed real plan developed for an urgent care center. In addition, the four appendices provide suggestions on 1) how to develop an advertisement; 2) how to use marketing consultants; 3) integrating computers into health marketing; and 4) working with the media. These two sections are important as more and more health organizations begin to advertise as a form of marketing strategy, many organizations require the utilization of external marketing resources such as consultants, become sophisticated with marketing-related microcomputer systems, and deal with the media on a wider level.

Of course, this text is a guideline for developing a strategic marketing plan. There are many more literary resources that should be used by the marketer or administrator. It is hoped that this text has proven to be a key resource for assisting your marketing endeavors.

CASE EXAMPLE:
JOB DESCRIPTION OF A VICE-PRESIDENT
OF MARKETING FOR A COMMUNITY HOSPITAL

The following provides a detailed example of the job description for the Vice-President of Marketing for a typical community hospital. Of course the size of the hospital and budget constraints will expand or contract the human resources related to this description. This description is based on a composite from various marketing directors around the country.

Position title: Vice-President of Marketing, Stratmore Hospital

Reports to: Chief Executive Officer

Other positions on same line of authority:
Vice-President of Finance
Vice-President of Patient Care

Supervises:

Director of Public Relations
Director of Planning
Director of Fund Raising
Director of Patient/Community Relations
Director of New Service Planning (including Marketing Research)

Basic function:

Responsible for planning, directing, controlling, and coordinating the overall marketing activities of the hospital in order to meet or exceed organizational goals within approved constraints established by the Board of Directors.

Adjunct reporting areas:

Directs the marketing subcommittee of the Board of Directors.

Directs the Organizational Marketing Committee.

Works closely with general counsel and medical staff to insure hospital's marketing activities are conducted in accordance with regulations, and ethical and medical standards.

Works closely with Vice-President of Finance and Vice-President of Patient Services.

Works closely with operating managers of departments and service centers to insure effective coordination between day-to-day operations and marketing goals, objectives, strategies, and tactics.

Major responsibilities:

I. Coordinates all marketing, public relations, planning, fund raising, and community relations functions for the hospital.

II. Develops for approval by the CEO and Board of Directors short- and long-term marketing goals and objectives.

III. Develops for approval by the board and CEO a short- and long-term marketing plan for the hospital.

IV. Coordinates the overall strategic plan for the organization including planning for financial, organizational, human resource, and marketing goals and objectives.

V. Coordinates decisions related to service design, access to care, service pricing, and promotional activities (four P's of marketing mix).

VI. Directs the development of strategies and tactics for achievement of goals related to:

expansion
community outreach

new service development
service mix composition
media selection
pricing policies
reimbursement contingencies
promotional scheduling
image and positioning of services, etc.

VII. Directs the execution of approved marketing and strategic plans.

VIII. Reviews and controls hospital performance relating:
revenue performance against plan
competitive position in the marketplace
market share by service type and target group
utilization rates
image and community perception rates

IX. Coordinates the collection of marketing research and audit information for identifying target groups and trend analysis.

X. Keeps abreast of all key economic and market environmental changes affecting the hospital and the industry.

XI. Maintains a strong network with other marketing directors, local and national marketing associations, legislative and regulatory agencies, competitors, consumer and special interest groups, general community leaders, health and medical associations and unions, medical providers affiliated with the hospital, and the advisory and board members.

XII. Represents the hospital at appropriate industry, trade, and community functions.

XIII. Coordinates the development of new services based on market analysis and within local regulatory constraints.

XIV. Directs and coordinates all fund raising activities related to the Director of Fund Development, Board of Directors, advisory groups, and volunteers.

XV. Coordinates internal training for staff, board members, and medical providers on their roles in marketing their services and the hospital.

XVI. Maintains strong relations with key members of the medical staff who play an administrative or political role related to potential effectiveness of marketing activities.

XVII. Insures the hospital's strategic plan and marketing plan is in tune with industry trends and market opportunities.

XVIII. Coordinates all contracting and negotiation for the formulation of new delivery modes, i.e., preferred provider organization, health maintenance organization, mergers, etc.

XIX. Directs all administrative planning and marketing committees.

XX. Directs all advertising campaigns with appropriate marketing resources such as advertising agencies, consultants, planning firms, marketing research organizations, etc.

Chapter 9

Condensed Sample Marketing Plan

The following marketing plan is based upon a composite of several different marketing plans the author has developed using the systematic framework described in the prior chapters. The sample plan is meant to be a reference and a guideline for any type of health organization or program which is developing a marketing plan. I have referred the reader to select chapters which describe the particular section being discussed. Therefore, it is important for the reader to remember that it is a generic reference and the methodology is applicable to many different types of health and human services. It is an edited version of a formal plan. Most plans can range from about twenty pages to over 100 depending upon the amount of research and analysis. The most common question I receive from health professionals who are preparing a marketing plan is related to the fact that they have never seen an actual plan. It is hoped the plan will alleviate some of these needs but no plan should be exactly duplicated as each organization has unique marketing characteristics and needs. I have selected one of the most exciting areas in health care delivery, that of ambulatory care. The urgent care format of delivery is widespread throughout the country and is multiplying in the form of emergicenters, convenience care centers, express care centers, and same day surgery centers.

MARKETING PLAN FOR ENTERPRISE HOSPITAL'S URGENT CARE CENTER (CARING CENTER)

EXECUTIVE SUMMARY AND BACKGROUND

Enterprise Hospital is a general acute hospital located in San Francisco County, California. The hospital is a private not-for-profit health care institution which traces its lineage to 1889. Enterprise Hospital encompasses the 230-bed acute care hospital as well as a full range of ambulatory, ancillary, and rehabilitation programs under its Enterprise Hospital Division. As a teaching hospital, Enterprise also includes a large intern, resident, and fellowship program along with the associated staff faculty members. The majority of the faculty have their private offices in the attached Enterprise Medical Building.

On December 1, 1982 Enterprise Hospital purchased the Sacramento Health Clinic located two blocks from the main hospital, which had been in operation for less than two months. As ambulatory care services have materialized as a progressive new form of health delivery during the past decade, Enterprise decided to convert the clinic into an urgent care center. November 1983 witnessed the opening of the new Urgent Care Center under the name Caring Center. This transition to opening an urgent care center was a response to an overcrowded emergency room and a mechanism for providing same-day appointments for non-emergency care. It was hoped the Caring Center would improve access to care for the hospital's service area, prevent misappropriate usage of the emergency room, provide a new revenue source for the hospital, and lower the cost of health care to the community. In addition, the medical staff developed a keen interest in the urgent care center as a potential source of private referrals to them. The rationale for this interest was that a patient who came to the Caring Center probably would not have a regular physician, might need specialized services, and would theoretically be referred to a participating specialist by the Center.

As with most hospitals in the same geographic area, economic conditions have changed for Enterprise Hospital. Current projected inpatient demand is insufficient; increased competition from local hospitals, HMOs, Group Practices, and Preferred Provider Organizations have materialized; the growth of the local population has stagnated; the hospital's aging medical staff may threaten long-term financial growth; and government changes in reimbursement for Medicare and Medicaid are starting to have some impact on recovering the hospital's cost of care. These trends plus the future outlook for a greater prospective reimbursement emphasis by public and private insurance sources have stimulated the hospital's board of directors and administration to investigate alternative new service development including a consulting division, a same-day surgery center, acquisition of a long-term care center, and a wellness program for contracting with private businesses. Of course, one of their decisions related to this investigation was the opening of Caring Center. At this point in time, the Center has been open for eleven months and is not living up to expectations. Thus, the hospital's board has decided to hire a marketing consultant to develop a marketing plan specifically designed to market the Caring Center for Enterprise Hospital. The following marketing plan is being presented to the Board of Directors of Enterprise Hospital on October 17, 1984 as a potential guideline for the hospital's endeavors in marketing the Caring Center. The plan has been developed over a three-month time frame and can be initially implemented during the next twelve months through the majority of the 1985 calendar year.

ORGANIZATIONAL AND MARKETING MISSIONS

(Please see Chapter 3 for reference on developing organizational and marketing missions.)

The stated mission of Enterprise Hospital is to 1) provide excellence in medical care within a teaching environment, 2) improve the standards of medical care in the San Francisco area, 3) provide an environment suitable for the training of future physicians and clinical research, and 4) offer a broad range of basic and specialized hospital services on an inpatient and outpatient basis.

The mission of Caring Center is to provide a wide range of ambulatory care services to the population of San Francisco County on a non-emergency basis and to complement the services offered by Enterprise Hospital.

The mission of the marketing plan for Enterprise Hospital's Caring Center is to increase the Center's client base, expand the utilization of Enterprise Hospital's main services, develop an active referral network for the hospital's medical staff, and to let the community become aware of a new alternative mode of care.

MARKETING GOALS AND OBJECTIVES

(Please refer to Chapter 3 for reference on developing marketing goals and objectives.)

Goal 1: To expand the number of clients using the Center.
Objective 1: To increase the Center's utilization by 50% by the end of 1985's calendar year.

Objective 2: To expand the mix of patients to the Center from existing markets and new markets.

Objective 3: To increase the proportion of private-pay patients by 25% by the end of 1985.

Objective 4: To increase the number of business employees using the Center by 100% by the end of 1985.

Objective 5: To attract new target groups to the Center: commuters, local students, and small business owners.

*   *   *

AUTHOR'S NOTE: This audit is only 10% of its original length for editing purposes. Certain categories discussed in Chapter 4 have been deleted as have the graphs and tables. However, it does provide a good survey of the major systematic approach to an audit for the reader. Please see Chapter 4 for a complete analysis on putting an audit together.

*   *   *

MARKETING AUDIT

Macroenvironmental Information:

Population Trends

The population of San Francisco county exceeds 680,000 people. While the U.S. and California have experienced steady growth in population, San Francisco's trend is declining. For example, California's population from 1970 to 1980 has increased over 7%. Meanwhile, San Francisco's population has declined by an average of 1.3% per year from 1970 to 1980. This decline is due to a migration out of the primary San Francisco County into Alameda, Contra Costa, Marin, and Peninsula areas. The greatest migration out of San Francisco has occurred from the southern and central sections of the County. The population projection through 1990 is for a slowing of this population decline to approximately .7%/year.

Ethnic Background

San Francisco's racial composition has undergone significant change since 1970. The most dramatic change has been the increase in the Chinese and decrease in the Caucasian population groups.

The second biggest increase has been the Spanish-speaking population. These trends appear to be forecasted to continue through 1990.

Age

San Francisco in comparison to the U.S. in 1977 is shown below:

	LESS THAN 14	15-24	25-44	45-64	+65
U.S.:	16%	18.6%	31.7%	22.4%	11.3%
S.F.:	17.1%	19.1%	25.5%	23.4%	14.9%

The major trend of the population shift has been a steadily increasing senior citizen marketplace.

Sexual Breakdown

There are over 340,000 males and 341,000 females in San Francisco County with the median age of 33.2 years for males and 35.3 years for females.

Family Unit

S.F. County has 140,490 total families with a total number of households over 300,000. The mean number of people per household is 2.2.

Occupation and Income

The main occupational source in San Francisco is services. The three main occupation groups are retail, finance, and human services. The median adult income in S.F. is over $14,000 per year.

Health Status

Heart disease, cancer, stroke, and accidents represent primary causes for death for over 70% of the population in the county. Cancer, heart disease, and accident rates are higher than national or state averages. S.F. also is represented by the highest mortality rates of influenza, pneumonia, cirrhosis, and suicide.

Commute

The majority of workers in S.F. commute from Alameda, Contra Costa, and Marin Counties.

Shopping Centers/Tourism

There are four major shopping centers near the Care Center. Tourism is S.F.'s largest industry with over 3½ million visitors per year.

Housing/Local Industry

The average San Francisco home is priced over $130,000 and in excess of 100 of the largest 500 corporations have offices in or near San Francisco.

Access

There is excellent public transportation in S.F. and there is good highway access from the East, North, and South Bay Areas. The Care Center is not near a major freeway but is near excellent bus and BART transportation.

Microenvironmental Information:

Clinic Utilization During First Eleven Months

The largest proportion of patients have been between the ages of 18-40 (53%); male (59%); Private Insurance (34%), Medi-Cal (24%), and Private Pay (17%); 60% claimed not having a family physician of which 47% were specifically referred to an Enterprise staff member; heaviest usage occurred between 12-6 pm (57%); 81% of visits were made on Mondays-Wednesdays; 41% were Caucasians; 80% resided in homes; and 75% were employed. In addition, 100% of the clients are derived from S.F. County. Of the local hospital area's population 45% is over the age of 65 but this group counted for only 9.5% of the clinic's activities. The largest proportion of users were in the 18-40 age group; and the largest proportion of clients are walk-ins.

Competitors

There are eight emergency rooms and three other urgent care centers within a two mile radius of the Care Center. The closest one is the Weston Urgent Care Center ½ mile on the west side of the city. In terms of access, the Care Center is less than 100 yards from the Enterprise Emergency Room. Competition is fierce for emergency, outpatient, and ambulatory patients. In addition, there are over 12 large group practices and one minor emergency clinic serving the same area as the Care Center. It appears that three other local hospitals are planning new urgent care centers within the next year.

Market Share

The local HSA estimates that Enterprise Hospital has a 6% share of the marketplace within S.F. County. This ranks them the sixth largest hospital in terms of serving patients out of thirteen hospitals in the county.

Finances/Utilization/Staffing

The Care Center currently has a $1,000,000 yearly budget. Break-even has been estimated at 42 patient visits/day. The current utilization rate is 21 patients/day. The Care Center can efficiently handle a maximum of 65 patients/day with current staffing of four physicians, five nurses, and four clerical assistants for a twelve-hour operating day. The Center has a sliding scale fee schedule with the average client paying $34/visit.

Psychographics

There is currently no survey information which has been collected for service, lifestyle, psychological, and behavioristic profiles. From a short survey of 10% of the current patients, a brief profile of the typical client was: satisfied with service; appreciative of the courteous service by the staff and short waiting times; young and quite athletically active; upwardly mobile; and uses the clinic routinely four times a year due to strong loyalty.

Current Marketing Activity

Almost no marketing has been done for the Care Center since it opened. Only activities were: brochures sent to 5% of the residents in a five mile radius; an open house for medical staff; and word of mouth referrals that were expected to stimulate growth. The director of public relations at the hospital allocates about two hours per week to the Center.

Demand Analysis

Currently 30% of the users are referrals from existing clients. The survey of the general local population indicated that 92% of 3,000 people surveyed in a five mile radius of the Center were unaware of the Center but indicated that they might consider using it after becoming familiar with it. This survey also indicated that 41% did not have a family physician. The survey did indicate that 75% were not satisfied with their current medical services.

Stage of Life Cycle

Given its current utilization pattern, potential demand in the community, and lack of marketing, the Center is still in the early stages of the Growth Phase.

Physician Attitudes

The physician staff from the return of 24% of the surveys sent to the medical staff of Enterprise Hospital indicated the staff had significant desire to see the Center prosper for future referrals, definitely were apprehensive about advertising the Center or using more sophisticated marketing techniques, did not fully understand the role of marketing, and blamed the administration for the Center's not being prosperous. The four physicians assigned to the Center were very enthused and ambitious about the Center and were, of course, most interested that quality medical care be provided. They were a lot more receptive to using other marketing techniques for the Center.

Audit Conclusion

Opportunities: It is apparent that the Care Center has the potential for complementing Enterprise Hospital; may provide new sources of patients for the hospital and the medical staff; can fill a niche in the marketplace for providing ambulatory services to the public; is off to a good start despite the fact that very little marketing has been done; appears to have strong loyalty of those clients who have used the service; has potential in new segments of the S.F. County area plus other counties; possesses a strong financial backing; is well staffed; has good access; is priced reasonably; has the backing of administration and the Board of Directors; has a quality-oriented, long-standing, and competitively strong hospital as a foundation; and needs to explore new service development such as same-day surgery.

Risks: The risks which the Center needs to address include the current and future competition for the same client base; the need to attract more support from the medical staff; a stagnant population growth; attempts to attract clients from other counties in which additional competition is materializing; sensitivity to the medical staff's and board's attitudes about marketing; lack of marketing personnel for implementation; and the need to diversify its referral sources due to a total dependence on S.F. patient origin.

MARKET SEGMENTATION

(Please see Chapter 5 for reference on the segmentation process.)

Based on the audit information and analysis, the following segments are currently or have the potential to interact with the Care Center:

1. All residents in the county of San Francisco;
2. Residents in other counties in the Bay Area;
3. Hospital's medical staff;
4. Other physicians in the community;
5. Employees of private clinics;
6. Local businesses;
7. The senior care marketplace;
8. Other health agencies and organizations in the community;
9. Commuters and transportation centers;
10. Media;
11. Police/Fire Departments/Ambulance Services;
12. Community associations and groups;
13. Insurance companies;
14. Schools and students;
15. The population group without a physician;
16. The loyal group (30% referrals by existing patients);

17. All current clients;
18. The Hospital staff, administration, and board;
19. Other health institutions in the community;
20. 18-40 year old service workers;
21. Tourists;
22. Religious groups;
23. Industrial injury groups;
24. Workman compensation groups;
25. Downtown white collar workers;
26. New San Francisco residents;
27. Apartment dwellers near Center;
28. Hotels and motels;
29. Rent-a-car centers;
30. Immigration offices;
31. Singles: heterosexual and homosexual groups;
32. Airline agents;
33. S.F. Chamber of Commerce and Information Bureaus;
34. Travel associations such as car clubs;
35. Medical interns and nursing students in local professional schools;
36. Day care centers in the city;
37. Shoppers/department stores/boutiques;
38. Specific ethnic groups: Spanish, Chinese, etc.;
39. Conventions;
40. Local government workers;
41. Construction workers;
42. Local Realtors and bankers.

MARKET TARGETING

(Please refer to Chapter 5 for reference on market targeting.)

Of the segments identified in the prior section, the primary and secondary target groups which deserve the most attention can be prioritized. The primary and secondary targets are being limited initially to ten target groups for the sake of length.

Primary Targets

The primary targets will merit our initial marketing strategies as they concentrate on large segments of the Center's publics which can provide quick returns on the Center's marketing investment. In many cases a formal cost-benefit study comparing the main segments can be very useful in prioritizing these target groups.

1. Commuters and workers in the financial district in service industries;
2. General population in San Francisco;
3. Qun (hospital and care center medical providers and staff);
4. Other health organizations in the County of San Francisco.

Secondary Targets

These target groups will be addressed after the initial strategies are implemented and evaluated for the primary target groups. They can also be utilized as back-up groups in case the primary groups are not as effective as desired.

1. Local residents without a family physician;
2. Local businesses;
3. Other medical providers in the community: i.e., physicians, dentists, therapists, etc.
4. Residents of other counties;
5. Fire Dept./Police Dept./Ambulance services;
6. Tourists;
7. Senior citizens in community.

MARKET POSITIONING

(Please see Chapter 6 for reference on market positioning.)

In marketing the Center the strategies can be directed to making the Center unique in the minds of the consumers and medical providers. The major perceptions of the Center which are most promising are positioning the Center as:

1. "The" all-purpose ambulatory care Center in San Francisco;
2. A convenient, easily accessible, Center;
3. A Center which will save clients money on not having to stay overnight in the main hospital;

4. The Center which maintains the quality care and mission of the hospital;
5. A way for patients to avoid the emergency room when it is not a serious problem;
6. The family physician for many clients who do not possess one;
7. The Center which has excellently trained and personable physicians, nurses, and staff;
8. Not a competitor to the emergency room but a complement to it and better in terms of time, money, access, convenience, and comfort;
9. Equal if not better qualified to handle non-threatening illnesses and injuries;
10. A Center which is safe and backed by the excellent facilities and services of the hospital;
11. An innovator in providing medical care;
12. Better coordinator with the patient's regular doctor (i.e., medical record sent to primary physician after visit);
13. The Center which provides individual attention and care;
14. "One stop shopping" for minor and intermediate services;
15. An information center for other human resources in the community;
16. Having the positioning statement: "The complete medical service Center where no appointment is needed, the doctor is always available, and the caring never ceases"; or "Caring Center: the emergency room alternative for you and your family";
17. Not just for emergencies but for routine medical care—colds, flu, aches, and pains.

MARKET STRATEGIES AND TACTICS

(Please see Chapter 7 for reference on developing marketing strategies and tactics.)

The following sample strategies and tactics are being developed to satisfy *Goal #1* and *Objectives 1 & 2* related to increasing the number of clients utilizing the Care Center and is directed to the main target groups of commuters, local residents, and medical staff of the hospital. Strategy #4 is presented as an array of different tactics to satisfy various goals and target groups. It is important to remember that actual public relations activities are tactics and are interwoven into these tactical examples.

Strategy #1: Promote the Care Center through advertisement, education, public relations, direct mail, and personal selling.

Tactics: Targeted to Commuter and General Public

1. Develop an article on emerging trends in urgent care centers with Care Center as the key case study.
2. Develop an advertisement in the local newspaper which is most widely read by commuters.
3. Arrange to have some of the Center's doctors on discussion shows in town.
4. Develop a thorough brochure which can be distributed through the mail for residents of local areas.
5. Have an open house for the public.
6. Possibly arrange a supplement to be placed in utility bills or corporate pay checks.
7. Have a series of personality talks at the Center for the public.
8. Have give-a-ways such as stickers, brochures, or flyers at the open house or for each client who visits the Center.
9. Check on road signs near the Center.
10. Take out ads on the morning commute radio stations.
11. Take out ads on public transportation with tear-out coupons.
12. Develop an ongoing newsletter to be mailed to residents.

Strategy #2: Communicate with hospital medical staff for reciprocal benefits.

Tactics: Targeted to Hospital and Center Medical Staff

1. Meet with family practitioners, pediatricians, and specialists and give a little educational session on marketing and the potential for referrals from the Center and indicate that no significant drop in emergency room visits should occur.
2. Discuss the importance of evening and weekend coverage for their patients.
3. Show examples of quality promotion tools for the Center with which the medical staff would be proud to be associated.

4. Have the medical staff meet and talk with the four main physicians in the Center.
5. Develop a newsletter to keep the medical staff up-to-date on Center activities.

Strategy #3: Develop a referral process from other health organizations.

Tactics: Targeted to Community Health Programs

1. Send personalized letters and brochures to administrators and clinicians in other hospitals, long-term care institutions, human service agencies, etc. Invite them to tour the facility.
2. Have an open house specifically for professionals.
3. Ask for advertising or announcement space in their newsletters or journals which go out to the public or their employees.
4. Make sure every human service organization in the county receives a copy of the newsletter.
5. Make sporadic on-site visits to other human service organizations to communicate in person and show an interest in their programs as well.

Strategy #4: Develop a referral mechanism from many different sources (miscellaneous tactics for the reader's reference).

Tactics: Targeted to Many Different Segments

1. Continually obtain new resident listings and mail brochures.
2. Send letters and brochures or in person discuss Care Center with apartment owners and realtors.
3. Talk with large hotel/motel managers about posting brochures or working out an arrangement for discounts for their guests.
4. Talk with employee benefits directors of local corporations about allowing some information to be directed to employees.
5. Set up booths at conventions or trade shows holding their meetings in San Francisco.
6. Call each patient 24 hours after service is provided.
7. Maintain files for sending out birthday and Christmas cards, etc. to patients or local businesses.
8. Contact department store managers about having posters or brochures about the clinic placed in high-traffic areas.

9. Contact local businesses about referral sources.
10. Provide free bus passes for public transportation for those potential clients who do not have cars.
11. Arrange for parking discounts in local lots.
12. Encourage repeat visits by offering discounts or family packages.
13. Advertise in airline journals and at travel agencies.
14. Get the physicians and staff involved in local social clubs, gatherings, or events.
15. Have some of the staff publish articles in health journals.
16. Arrange for Center physicians to make home visits to those patients who cannot make it to the Center.
17. Contract with a transportation firm for greater access for incapacitated patients.
18. Concentrate on nursing homes and board and care facilities in the vicinity for elderly clients.
19. Hire staff who are bilingual in Chinese or Spanish.
20. Develop a community board consisting of representation of local groups, businesses, and the general population.
21. Develop strong relationships with local and state medical and health associations, lobbyist groups, and consulting firms for referrals.
22. Develop a strong tie to United Way since they make a considerable number of referrals to clinics.
23. Investigate the use of appropriate billboards for advertisement.
24. Advertise in cultural journals such as ACT, Opera, and Symphony programs.
25. Develop a board subcommittee in marketing.
26. Since ancillary services will benefit considerably from the Center, develop a strong marketing orientation by these staff members for the Center.
27. Contact local Social Security officials for potential referrals.
28. Possibly offer major employers an initial free physical exam for their employees if contracting can be negotiated.
29. Explore preferred provider, HMO, IPA, etc. delivery modes for the Center.
30. Develop good working relations with local Blue Cross and Blue Shield Associations.
31. Patient and public surveys should be initiated to monitor effectiveness and community lifestyle and values.

32. Make sure a quality yellow pages ad is in place under "health," "clinic," and "emergency care."
33. Contact professional associations before they come to San Francisco for a convention for an inclusion in their program packages about the Center.
34. Advertise in KEY journals which are used in most cities to provide visitors with information about a city.
35. Contact immigration offices and travel agencies for a location to provide immunization shots.
36. Contact local unions about distributing information to their members.
37. Work with workman compensation agencies and insurance plans for potential referrals.
38. Contact local recreation departments and centers.
39. Send out periodical press releases emphasizing the uniqueness of the new service to the press.
40. Visit and distribute materials at mobile home parks in the area.
41. Contract with heavily visited restaurants in the area for shoppers, tourists, and white collar workers' information brochures or posters to be made available.

NOTE: Industrial and occupational medical services are becoming a major boost to urgent care centers. Therefore, marketing to industrial medicine clients is becoming important as companies have seen their health insurance premiums increase by 200-300%. Businesses are definitely observing urgent care centers as a possible way to reduce these costs. In addition, marketing to industry provides urgent care centers with access to large groups of patients, such as members of HMOs or PPOs. For example, several urgent care centers in Seattle have over 400 companies under informal contract and 16,000 employees under formal PPO contracts. A great strategy for this group is to land one of the largest companies, and then others will follow. Credibility by association can be a great strategy for these types of centers. Then if employees are satisfied, a multiplier impact can occur with their families and friends. In addition, it is important not to overlook the hundreds of small businesses that are present in most areas. It is also important for urgent care centers to not assume they know what businesses want in health services. Don't develop brochures before surveying your target markets! Businesses also want quick feedback on employees. For example, they want centers to call and provide a status report within the same day of the visit, and of course, they want their employees to return to work as soon as possible. In addition, having a hospital as a 24-hour backup to the urgent care center is an attraction versus the free-standing center. It is important to decide what the center should really offer; what it is capable of offering; what businesses want you to offer for their employees; and how well the center can meet this demand. Urgent care centers have only recently begun to scratch the surface of this potentially very large segment of the marketplace.

IMPLEMENTATION SCHEDULE

DATE	ACTIVITY
January, 1985	Organize marketing department with a director of marketing and subcommittee of board on marketing.
February, 1985	Begin developing meetings with medical providers and staff of the center and hospital.
March, 1985	Begin developing public relations materials: brochures, flyers, ads, posters, etc.
April, 1985–May, 1985	Initiate open houses for staff, other medical providers, public, and other health organizations.
June, 1985	Initiate visits to local businesses, unions, health organizations, and social groups.
July, 1985	Initiate first phase of advertising in newspapers, radio, newsletters, etc.
August, 1985	***(Initiate cost-benefit study for control system for first six months of plan implementation.)

DATE	ACTIVITY
September, 1985	Begin mailings to local residents, businesses, etc.
October–December, 1985	Begin implementing remaining first phase of strategies and tactics.
January, 1986	***(Initiate second control evaluation for second six months of implementation phase. Lay framework for updating plan for second calendar year and implementing second phase of strategies and tactics.)

CONTROL SYSTEMS

(Please refer to Chapter 8 on developing a control system.)

Two formal evaluations will be made in August, 1985 and January, 1986 for measuring cost-effectiveness of marketing strategies and tactics versus expected marketing goals and objectives. In other words, we need to specifically find out if we are satisfying the objectives of the marketing plan:

1. Have we increased the number of clients by 50%?
2. Have the number of private-pay patients increased by 25%?
3. Have we expanded the number of sources and mix of clients?
4. Have the number of business referrals increased by 100%?

If not, then we need to revamp different components of the plan, for example:

1. Change targets to secondary groups;
2. Implement different tactics;
3. Re-evaluate the orchestration of the components of the marketing mix;
4. Re-examine the realism of the marketing goals and objectives;
5. Initiate some new surveys to measure psychographics; and

6. Measure which tactics are more effective than others and put more emphasis on them.

ORGANIZATIONAL STRUCTURE OF MARKETING THE CARE CENTER

(Please refer to Chapter 8 for information on organizational structure.)

1. Hire a full-time director of marketing for the hospital. Initially allocate 10 hours per week of his/her time to the Center for first year.
2. Have the director of public relations and the director of fund development report to the director of marketing; 10 hours per week for first year report to Center.
3. After twelve months hire a 20-hour part-time marketer for the Center who would report to the director of marketing for the hospital; drop hours of director of marketing to five and public relations director to five.
4. The director of marketing will have direct access to the director of the Care Center and its staff.
5. The director of marketing will have direct access to the director of finance, the hospital's board, and legal counsel.
6. Formulate a subcommittee of the hospital board for marketing of which the director of marketing would be a member.
7. Organize a community relations committee for the Center which would be directed by the director of the Center and the director of marketing.

MARKETING BUDGET FOR CARE CENTER IN 1985

(Please refer to Chapter 8 for the marketing budget process.)

Total budget for the center is $1,000,000. An initial request for additional sums for marketing is as follows:

Labor: Implementation and Control of Plan

10 hours/week of Dir. of Mkt....	$12,000
10 hours/week of Dir. of Public Rel....	$8,000
Administrative/secretarial support...P/T	$5,000
Total	$25,000

Materials

Typeset, Printing, Xeroxing of Brochures, Flyers, Posters...		$7,000
Advertising development fees, ad agency, placement fees, rental space...		$15,000
	Total	$22,000

Implementation Costs

Mailing Lists Purchase...		$1,000
Mail Order House for Stuffing, Posting of Mailings...		$5,000
Postage...		$10,000
	Total	$16,000

Misc. Expenses

Travel (mileage, car rental, air fare, parking, etc....		$3,000
Estimated rough budget for first year of implementation of marketing plan...	Total	$66,000

The first year of marketing can be the most important. Therefore, the budget presented is a little more than 6% of the Care Center's total budget. This can be a very common investment during the first year if long-term results are expected. A range for any center of this type should be a minimum of 2-3% to a maximum of 7-8%. A guideline can be 3-4% of the Center's total budget after year 1.

SUMMARY

The reader has just completed surveying a real marketing plan. The optimum method for using the plan as a learning tool would be to read the text in sequence, then survey the marketing plan, and refer back to select chapters for guidelines. All of the materials presented in this plan will change according to the service being marketed, but the systematic format can be followed for the development of a successful marketing plan.

The next section of appendices supplies specific information on four important areas: 1) developing an advertisement, 2) suggestions for utilizing marketing consultants effectively, 3) using computers in health marketing, and 4) working with the media.

Appendix A:
The Fundamentals of Developing
an Effective Advertisement
for Health Care Organizations

INTRODUCTION

It wasn't too long ago that health professionals considered advertising unnecessary to increase or maintain business. More importantly, they were restrained by their professional organizations from using ads. But these attitudes and barriers have quickly changed and the trend toward advertising by health organizations and professionals is expanding. Unfortunately, most health administrators, planners, and marketers are not experienced or educated in developing advertisements for their organizations. Since astute marketing, advertising, and public relations techniques are no longer elective management tools for health professionals, this section is being presented as a basic reference for developing a more effective advertisement. However, it must be understood that advertising is only one tool of marketing strategies, but it will be a key option as part of marketing plans in the future.

A major marketing association has estimated that health care will be spending in excess of $500 million per year by 1990 for advertising their products and services, with hospitals, clinics, and group practices being the largest spenders. In fact, in 1984 over $50 million was spent just on television advertising by health organizations, up from just $1 million in 1978. As an example, it is estimated that over 25% of all practicing dentists now advertise in different media channels. Some of the biggest advertisers have been proprietary chains such as Schick-Shadel, Advanced Health Systems, Comprehensive Care Corporation, and the American Dental Council.

All of this pressure to advertise has occurred due to the awareness that oversaturated marketplaces exist, especially in metropolitan health markets, and that competition is here to stay. In addition, the advent of newer forms of health delivery systems such as clinics, preferred provider organizations, independent practice associations, emergicenters, urgent care centers, and service franchises have expanded the need for communicating effectively and quickly to our target groups through advertising. The constraints placed on the reimbursement systems have supported this trend toward seeking new service development and more effective marketing strategies.

It is important to remember that advertising can be subject to scrutiny under the FTC, FCC, state laws, rate review systems, and professional association standards. All professional advertising and promotion was altered by a landmark ruling on June 27th, 1977, by the U.S. Supreme Court in the case of John R. Bates and Van O'Steen versus the state bar of Arizona. The marketer needs to carefully check with local professionals' guidelines and their legal counsel before initiating any advertising campaign. However, the legal risks involved need not deter health care organizations from engaging in proper and effective competitive advertising. From the First Amendment to the U.S. Constitution, advertising is viewed as commercial speech and a mechanism to disseminate information to consumers. However, the legal aspects of all advertising campaigns require attention in order to prevent any significant long-term reactionary problems.

ROLE OF ADVERTISING IN MARKETING

There will be greater pressure on health facilities and programs to advertise in the future. A lot of this pressure is based on the premise that, "Let's Advertise—Everyone Else Is!" It is important to remember that advertising, again, is only one tool of marketing and may or may not be appropriate for the particular situation.

Advertising is not a miracle worker. It can only guide people's perceptions of the health organization until they use it for the first time. Advertising is only one part of the communications mix, which may include phone calls, brochures, admittance procedures, follow-up, etc. Advertising can really do only one thing. *It can convince a logical prospect for a service to try it one time!* It can't sell to someone who has no basic need for the service and it cannot make a satisfied client or patient. It also cannot save a bad service. The best advertising can do is cause reasonable prospects to try a service. Advertising is a simple business and process. "Keep it simple" is a premise that I have seen fail. Because this premise is so simple, it becomes difficult because we tend to make believe that better advertisements have to be more and more informative and complex. However, advertising goals for health organizations should be related to:

I. Creating an awareness of the service or organization;
II. Positioning the service in the minds of the consumers as to the differences between the service and its competitors;
III. Educating the public as to the need for select services and the availability of these services;
IV. Creating referrals for the main services;
V. Stimulating the usage of the services for the first time;
VI. Assisting in the creation of an environment in which the clients and patients will quickly and effectively accept the services in the marketplace; and
VII. When appropriate, improving the financial viability of the health organization.

Health organizations cannot depend on advertising to provide a successful service. The delivery of the service must come through in order for advertising to be effective. Advertising can only bring a person to use a service once. If the service is poorly delivered, treatment is inadequate, or the person is overcharged, repeat business will not be forthcoming. The success of any marketing campaign is realizing the referral and advertising can only initiate the contact. In fact, word of mouth is credited with generating over 60% of all new clients and patients, while advertising generates 25%. In addition, all interactions and contacts between the staff and the clients should relay a consistent image or message of the organization as reflected in the advertising campaign.

Organizations also cannot expect miracle effects from an advertising campaign. It needs to be nurtured and refined over a long time frame so that constant improvement is seen rather than immediate jumps in utilization of the services. It will not occur over night.

There appears to be little evidence of false or misleading advertising by health care professionals. Actually, the majority of complaints comes from peers in the same profession rather than consumers. Most complaints lodged with the FTC were from other health professionals, and most of those ads demeaned the profession but were not considered misleading or false.

Health care advertising unquestionably is on the upswing. However, the application of the money being spent on advertising is often amateurish and ineffectual. For example, it has been estimated that over two-thirds of all medical and dental ads were created by the medical/dental professional. In fact, over 75% of ads for solo and group practices are created by the medical provider and they do not employ professionals in any capacity, including media placement specialists. The small budgets allocated to advertising account for much of this self-creativity trend. For instance, over 80% of all solo practitioners spend less than $15,000 a year and 64% are actually below this level.

Finally, it is important to remember that advertising is not for everyone. There are risks involved as in any business decision. However, effective ads can prove cost-beneficial. The early stages of feedback from those professionals and organizations who do advertise is favorable. From recent surveys, over 90% of those polled indicated that they were satisfied with the results and planned to advertise in the future. However, most of the feedback also indicated that they needed professional advice on 1) what to look for in developing an effective ad and 2) advice on media selection and placement. The next few sections outline the types of advertising strategies available and some basic tips on creating an effective advertisement for those who decide to develop their own or need to evaluate ads produced by external consultants or agencies.

TYPES OF ADVERTISEMENT AND MEDIA

There are many different forms of advertising. Some of these advertising channels include: television, radio, newspapers, journals, direct mail, yellow pages, shoppers/pennysavers, magazines, billboards, directories, transit space, posters, pens, memo pads, newspaper supplements, and others. The selection of the type of media channel depends mainly on:

1. the image the organization wants to promote;
2. the target groups it is addressing; and
3. the budgetary constraints.

A mix of these different media channels should be part of an advertising campaign in order to communicate with a large number of people. However, advertising needs to be sufficiently concentrated and repetitive in order to be effective in getting people to try the service. It has been proven that a person comes into contact with an advertisement four to five times before he/she tries the service. It is preferable to fund one media sufficiently before adding a second. In other words, a recommendation would be to end up with a smaller segment of the market fully aware of the service and organization rather than a large segment or segments only a little aware. However, the media mix selection process is one which should be done by marketing professionals just as the mix of medical treatments for a patient requires professional medical advice!

FUNDAMENTALS IN WRITING
A SUCCESSFUL ADVERTISEMENT

The following six basic steps provide a base for developing an effective advertisement:

I. *Identify the target groups and their psychographic profile:* Creating an advertisement which will cause a prospect to try the service can be relatively easy. First of all, determine what you are trying to say as a basic message and identify the audience or target group to whom you are saying it. An underlying rule of advertising is to make sure the ad is developed to relate to the values and interests of your target groups. Developing a differentiated or concentrated approach to advertising can be more effective than an undifferentiated one. All of the auditing, segmenting, and targeting analysis comes into play for identifying primary and secondary targets. A special emphasis should be placed on the psychographic/ lifestyle analysis related to understanding the psychological, lifestyle, and behavioristic aspects of the potential consumer groups. Advertisements must relate to the consumer's values, perceptions, and interests. To make things easier always contact the newspaper, radio station, or TV channel where you are advertising to inquire whether they have completed some key demographic and psychographic profiles of their listeners or readers. For example, some local newspapers have some excellent profiles of their readership and subscribers which may assist in picking the right media channel and the most cost-beneficial target groups.

II. *Get attention:* Nobody is waiting anxiously in the community to read or hear your advertisement! In addition, most people are usually oversaturated with advertisements through print and other media channels. Your advertisement must get the attention of a consumer quickly and have a lasting effect. It has been proven that most people will spend no longer than five to ten seconds reading a print ad and fifteen seconds listening to an audio advertisement. Therefore, uniqueness through headlines, color, creative graphics, catchy slogans, or pictures must catch the attention of your reader or listener long enough for them to be interested in reading or listening to the rest of the ad. Again, this is especially important when, for example, the average American is exposed to over 30,000 television ads every year, *The New York Times* often carries 350 pages of advertisements on an average Sunday, and radio stations can offer 40 minutes in every hour to commercials.

III. *Demonstrate an advantage:* If we can get the attention of the reader or listener then the ad must answer the question, "What will this professional service do for me?" It is important to inform the consumer exactly how the service may impact them mentally, physically, on their state of well-being, level of self-respect, satisfaction, security, etc. The actual copy of the advertisement should be kept short but potent. In other words, explain in the ad how your service is unique and what positive outcome will be derived from trying it. There are different methods to communicate these ideas. For example, ads can use humor, present settings which approximate real life, have testimonials, present demonstrations, show solutions to problems, offer pitchmen and women, give specific reasons, and stimulate emotional ties to the service.

IV. *Prove the advantage:* After we identify the key advantage give some facts which prove the validity of the uniqueness. Facts may be necessary. For example, the ad can show the educational degrees of the professionals involved, the variety of services offered, the number of people successfully treated, the exact fees charged and payment mechanisms available, or even the time required to obtain the service. Use understatement because it carries more conviction than overstatement. "Always see the ad from the eyes of the consumer."

V. *Persuade people to take advantage:* It is important to make a quick but potent impression in the minds of the consumer. Portray what the service can do for them and how easily they can obtain it. For example, discuss access, pricing, parking, types of staff, payment plans available, or insurance coverage. Plan the ad to persuade your *toughest* target group. In other words, the ad should be addressed to attract even the most difficult group. If that group is attracted then the easier target groups will follow. Persuasion must get the potential consumer to the point they are *aware of the service, understand the need for it, and are potentially ready to use it.*

VI. *Call for action:* The ad must make the consumer take action. However, the ad should ask for the consumer to act in some way. There has to be some type of "do-something" statement in the ad which makes it simple, easy, specific, and special for the consumer to try the service for the first time. In other words, we may suggest that people call, send in a coupon, mail something to us, or come by and visit us. A traditional way has been to have an open house whereby people can come and check out the service before making any commitment.

These six basic steps can be used as a checklist when designing an advertisement. Since most ads will probably be designed by external marketing firms it is important to have the copy ready before the design and layout are developed. This requires the health organization to have the basic concept organized before sending it out to the agency. Discuss the concept carefully with the designers so they can have a guideline from which to develop a layout which communicates the organization's important ideas and services. An excellent source of communication for health organizations is radio advertising. Unfortunately, radio has become the Cinderella of advertising media, representing only 6% of total advertising in the United States. When getting the right message across on radio ads, there are four important ingredients:

1. Identify the name of the service early in the ad;
2. Repeat the name often;
3. Promise the listener a benefit for trying the service early in the ad; and
4. Repeat the ad often.

You have to get people to listen to your ad. Wake them up! Then talk to them! Get them involved! It is also important to make several ads as people quickly become bored with the same ad on the radio. However, there is truly very little accurate research on exactly which type of advertisement is the most cost-effective in actually increasing sales or bringing in clients and patients.

TYPES OF ADVERTISING AGENCIES

Advertising agencies are independent firms which develop and place ads in various media channels. There are thousands of advertising agencies in the country. The agency is mainly responsible for working with a client to 1) plan an advertising campaign for the health organization; 2) select and contract for the media in which they feel will produce cost-effective results; 3) prepare the advertising copy, layout, photography, and artwork; 4) produce the final ad in the format acceptable to the media channel; and 5) handle all transactionary and placement duties related to the ad in the media channel selected.

Advertising agencies range from small creative boutiques which only write copy to full range service agencies which can provide assistance in a wide range of marketing functions including research, planning, design, media selection, and strategy development. In picking among these types of agencies it is important to balance convenience and expertise. An agency which is local may supply convenience and knowledge of the local health marketplace. The national firm may be less convenient but may have more talented support staff. Unfortunately, there is no rating service which rates the quality of the services provided by advertising agencies. Therefore, it is important to ask for a list of prior or current clients who you can contact for evaluations. Some TV and radio stations will also sometimes supply the names of firms which have been easy or difficult to work with through the years. Feeling comfortable with the people at the agencies is just as important as finding one with the highest quality staff or resources.

ADVERTISING EXPENSES

Fees range dramatically for advertising agencies. For example, most agencies have averaged about 15-20% commission on media purchases and add on hourly charges for production costs and retainer fees. There is beginning to be some very creative pricing by agencies during recent years so negotiating with agencies is strongly recommended. For example, the fees may be based on 1) a fixed retainer that is estimated on the work to be performed plus retention of all commissions received; 2) a variable monthly rate depending upon the commissions received by the agency; and 3) an hourly rate based on the exact functions of copywriting, artwork, or layout.

Advertising on TV, radio, newspaper, billboards, or other media channels may be expensive. It is important to call the different TV stations or newspapers to compare fees as it ranges significantly among channels, size of the ad, frequency of the ad, and positioning of the ad according to the time it plays or days it is published or viewed. In other words, shop around and compare. Most health organizations spend a small amount on marketing, and even less on advertising. This budget allocation will continue to grow. Of course, it will never reach the levels of consumer product companies such as Proctor & Gamble˙ which spends more than $600,000,000 per year on advertising!

As a guideline, recent surveys by the Advertising Council indicate that service-oriented businesses spend an average of 3.5% of gross sales for advertising. Health care organizations are not even above 1% of gross revenues!

CONCLUSION

Creativity, not budget size, is vital to advertisements' becoming popular and effective. In an overcrowded marketplace marketers can become afraid to take chances. Marketing productivity is declining as we have tended to look for quick financial success rather than satisfying, long-range objectives. An advertising campaign must be creative and will involve some risk, whether it is financial or the fear of poor feedback from our peers. However, health organizations must establish the climate of willingness to change and tolerate risk if you are to have innovation. In addition, pretesting is essential when creative ads are developed. People may perceive differently the message being delivered by the ad. It is important to pretest to see if the intended message is clear and understood by consumers and meets the objectives of the campaign and the organization. Pretesting must be done with people who are similar to those who will be listening or reading the advertisement in the long-run. Most health organizations are new to the concept of advertising. They are currently advertising similar to the statement by Will Rogers, "Advertising is like the rattling of a stick inside a swill-bucket." Gradually advertising will become more sophisticated and be a major new tool for health administrators and marketers.

If we can recap the basics of developing an effective advertisement, it is that any good ad must possess three ingredients:

1. Information about the service and its uniqueness;
2. A clear statement which expresses this advantage and relates to the target group; and
3. A creative and attention-getting presentation.

These three ingredients must be based on two premises: simplicity *and* believability. *The essential framework to express an advertisement is that an ad must have something to say and offer value and it should be expressed straight and simple.*

ADDITIONAL RESOURCES ON ADVERTISING

When it is necessary to acquire information for the preparation of an advertising budget, program, or media placement, seek out the *Rate & Data Service Directory.* SRDS Directories, of Skokie, Illinois, provides directories for rates in newspapers, business publications, consumer magazines, transit space, etc. These directories are typically available in most business libraries.

A second key directory is the *Ayer Directory of Publications,* Philadelphia, Pennsylvania, which has been published for over 100 years. It provides an in-depth look at thousands of newspapers, magazines, trade publications, college publications, etc.

A third source is advertising trade journals. Some of the more popular journals include:

Advertising Age
Adweek Magazine
Art Direction Magazine
Broadcasting Magazine
Marketing Communications

There are many of these types of reference journals.

A fourth area of resources is from seminars and workshops put on by colleges and marketing associations. For example, the American Marketing Association, Chicago, Illinois, has a subdivision titled Academy of Health Care Marketing, which produces excellent resources. The AMA also produces quality references on advertising. Most cities have local chapters of this organization. Some other key organizations for advertising resources include:

THE ADVERTISING CHECKING BUREAU, INC., Chicago,
Illinois
THE ADVERTISING COUNCIL, New York, N.Y.
ADVERTISING RESEARCH FOUNDATION, New York,
N.Y.
AMERICAN ADVERTISING FOUNDATION, Washington,
D.C.
ASSOCIATION OF NATIONAL ADVERTISERS, New
York, N.Y.
NEWSPAPER ADVERTISING BUREAU, New York, N.Y.
RADIO ADVERTISING BUREAU, New York, N.Y.

The Directory of Associations in most business libraries can provide current addresses and names for many other organizations which can provide excellent information on advertising.

EXAMPLE OF EXCELLENT ADVERTISING

(Special thanks to Barbara Brady at B&B Advertising and the Administrator of South Bergen Hospital for the contribution of their advertisements.)

South Bergen Hospital in Hasbrouck Heights, New Jersey, adopted an advertising campaign for its 40-bed facility in 1984. The hospital's reputation had been tarnishing due to an aging facility. Holy Names Hospital, a 370-bed local facility, began managing South Bergen Hospital and began a series of physical improvements to the facility.

B&B Advertising in Bogota, New Jersey, was hired to design an advertising campaign for 1) improving the image of the hospital; 2) demonstrating the hospital's innovative management; and 3) to demonstrate that the hospital was more than capable of serving the health needs of the local community.

B&B Advertising decided to concentrate on marketing South Bergen Hospital's 1) Senior Citizen Health Program; 2) Emergency Services; and 3) Podiatric Center. The agency decided on targeting their ads to the general public in the local community as well as to local doctors and podiatrists. The goals were to attract more people to the hospital as well as more physicians who might affiliate themselves with South Bergen Hospital. The ad campaign included a six-month program of quarter page ads that were also incorporated into a full-page advertisement stressing "The New South Bergen Hospital." The first series of quarter page ads stressed the Senior Citizen Health Program (see ad #1) and it appeared in three local newspapers for the month of June, 1984. During the first month of appearance over 40 new patients had joined the program!

The second series of ads featured the emergency care center and this series began during the month of July, 1984. An immediate increase in usage of the emergency room occurred in response to the ad (see ad #2).

A similar response was initiated by the placement of the third series of ads for the podiatric center at the hospital (see ad #3).

Analysis of Advertisement #1: Senior Citizen Health Program

As the reader scans the advertisement, there are some important strategies for communicating information which should be noted. Every step in developing the ad required a strategy to reach their original goals.

Identification of target groups: The target group was identified immediately 1) by the title of the program in bold face type and 2) through the use of a sketch of two senior citizens. The marketing approach in this instance is a concentrated one. The service matches a select group who can be marketed to with a unique marketing mix.

Getting attention: In the overcrowded marketplace, the ad was strategically placed and drew attention from readers. This attention is being garnished from the use of bold face in the title, name of the hospital, sketches, and graphic lines providing a boundary for the advertisement.

Demonstrate an advantage: Right off the top of the ad the reader sees that the center offers "One Stop Health Care" which indicates no need to see a variety of medical providers or clinics for the senior person's health needs. The following statement, "Where Our Patients Become Friends," continues to support the demonstration of an advantage in using this center. The advantage is being portrayed as one in which the senior citizen has trust in their center and use it as a long-term resource.

Prove the advantage: In the script next to the picture it indicates that the medical care is personalized, the staff is a caring one, and it offers special understanding for the senior citizen's health needs. The itemized list in the boxed graphics also proves the advantage through a continued list of advantages. The affiliation with Holy

ADVERTISEMENT #1.

Name Hospital in bold face complements the strategy to build trust and confidence which is so important in marketing to the senior group.

Persuasion to take action: The aggregate pieces of the advertisement emphasize trust, confidence, understanding of unique needs, information for access, and a continued approach to persuade the senior citizen to use the center.

Call for action: There is a direct call for action by the boxed information "Call: Monday-Friday, 8 a.m.–4 p.m." An interesting strategy is the extra graphic lines around this piece of information within the second larger box which is even within a third box around the whole ad. The telephone number in bold face at the bottom is as large as the name of the hospital. This is an indirect message to call.

The advertisement is informative, simple, and clear. It relates to its audience effectively and stimulates the reader to take notice. It is not flashy (which might turn off a senior citizen group), nor is it overly creative. It is an ad which is straight to the point, and thus, has been effective.

The only suggestions for improvement to make the ad even more effective would be to use a little less script, type for the script which is a little easier to read by the senior citizen group, and possibly a bolder approach to setting off the name of the service so that it stands out even more. Overall, the ad was very well done and proved to be highly cost-effective for the center and the hospital.

Analysis of Advertisement #2: Emergency Services

This ad was placed to attract more patients to use the hospital's emergency room while indirectly marketing the hospital in general. A different approach is used in this ad. First of all, the ad is dominated by a real photograph rather than a sketch. The picture significantly features a child and a doll: the child is a universality in marketing. It connotes sympathy, understanding, and caring. Many adults will be attracted to the ad because it parallels from a psychological perspective the aspect that when adults have accidents the disability makes them vulnerable like a child. There is a connotation of compassion. Immediately it puts the emergency service into a parental protective role and will take care of the adult, as well as the child, when the need arises. The child is taking care of her doll, just as the emergency room will take care of the adult.

There is also a difference in the ad in that there is no formal bold face used to emphasize the name of the service. The ad is more visual rather than interpretive. The connation of an emergency is to

use the service quickly without a lot of need for information. It is also targeted to multiple groups rather than to one as in the first ad. The information is brief, to the point, and effective.

The script is written to 1) relate to a wide variety of target groups; 2) offer an advantage through 24-hour service; 3) pull on the heart strings by persuading the reader to relate and take action; and 4) call for action through the boldface name of the hospital and telephone number. Simplicity and emotional stimulus are the key marketing strategies in this ad. Overall, the ad delivers its message. The only suggestion for improvement would be to rotate the picture to show other members of a family while the ad appears in the newspaper, highlight the phone number in larger print, and probably throw in some directions to get to the hospital. For instance, a little map in the corner might be helpful for people needing to know how to get to the hospital in a rush.

Analysis of Ad #3: Podiatry Center

This ad takes on an entirely different strategy. Here we have an ad which uses 1) sketches; 2) a medium amount of verbage; 3) a little humor; and 4) graphics positioning.

The emphasis in this ad is to have us relate to the problem of foot care, the runner, and the pun "You can't run away from." The second strategy is to relate to the runner. The ad is targeting to young, athletic, and probably, upwardly mobile adults. The ad is also cashing in on the tremendous trend in jogging and keeping fit. The boxed information is simple and uncluttered in its presentation. It is easy to read, catches your attention, and lets you know why you should use the service with 30 podiatrists (trust, quality care); same day service (urgent care mode, easy access, little time out of our busy schedule); most modern techniques (professional and advanced); local office appointments (easy access and convenience); screenings and consultations (preventive in mode of delivery); and most medical plans accepted (easy financial arrangements, little paper work).

The ad calls for action through the large bold face of the name of the hospital and the phone number along with the title "foot disorders." This beginning of the ad is important as it has been estimated by the Podiatry Association that over 80% of the adult population in the United States has some form of foot problem.

The only suggestion for improvement would be to better highlight the name of the service, "Podiatry Center"; indicate that it is a new and unique service; and expand the targeting to other groups of the adult population.

ADVERTISEMENT #3.

Overall, this is a very effective advertisement which 1) relates to its target group; 2) demonstrates a need and advantage; 3) attempts to persuade us to take advantage; and 4) calls us for action. It is also simple, clear, and easy to understand.

All three of these ads were directed to different target groups and designed to utilize various types of strategies and positioning. Yet they all have the common theme of marketing South Bergen Hospital effectively.

Appendix B:
How to Effectively Use
Health Marketing Consultants

INTRODUCTION

From my experiences in developing marketing plans for various types of health and human service organizations, the majority typically hire an outside consultant to assist in marketing their services. Most health administrators/providers do not generally possess experience in dealing with marketing consultants. Therefore, I want to share some key aspects of being cost-effective in utilizing marketing consultants for your health service. These key pitfalls and characteristics are based on my personal experiences as a marketing and management consultant, as well as those experiences of other consultants in the field of health services marketing. The insights shared by many marketing consultants around the country are deeply appreciated.

TYPES OF MARKETING CONSULTANTS

There are a variety of forms of consulting firms which provide some type of marketing services. These can be divided into the type of service they provide. For example, marketing services can be provided by:

— marketing planners
— public relations firms
— advertising agencies
— marketing research organizations
— fund raisers
— general management consultants
— communications and media firms

Each of these firms can provide specialized services or a full range of marketing functions.

Another form of marketing services is divided according to the size of the firm. For example, some consultants are self-employed as marketing consultants. Others work with marketing associates, operate small firms containing 2-3 partners with different expertises, are employed in large firms which may have 10 or more employees and have specialists for all needs, or are part-time consultants who work as educators or marketers full-time and consult on a part-time basis.

There is no one best form of a consulting firm. However, key criteria should be the amount of money you wish to budget for marketing and the amount of personal attention you wish to receive from the firm.

During recent years there has been a steady increase in the number of consulting firms having a component of marketing expertise. Competition among these firms has become keen. Many of them can be found in the yellow pages of the phone directory, by recommendation from local marketing associations, from referral by local health organizations, and in local better business bureaus or even some chambers of commerce. From personal experience, most health administrators do not shop around enough and accept services from consultants without extensive analysis.

PRICING THE MARKETING SERVICES

There are numerous methods that are utilized for setting consulting charges. For example, a consultant may work on a flat fee basis for specific activities and length of time. This flat fee can include a deferred payment mechanism. However, a flat fee usually does not include expenses such as travel, meals, or supplies.

Other consultants may require a minimum base fee with an incentive clause for the number of new clients that are brought into the organization. Some consultants may work on a total commission basis or on an hourly basis. There is tremendous flexibility in negotiating charges. Do not hesitate to barter to meet your marketing needs and operate within the organization's financial limitations. Setting a budget before signing a consulting contract is vitally important.

ACCESS TO THE CONSULTANT

The location of consultants varies. There are local firms which typically concentrate within the local marketplace. Some others work on a regional basis and can be located, for example, throughout a state. Then there are national firms which have offices in many major cities.

The key criteria is easy access to the consultant and convenience of meeting with them. For example, you may have a busy schedule which prohibits you from meeting with your consultants during the daytime. You may require access to the consultant during the evening or on weekends. Or you may desire to have the consultant physically present on a full-time basis. During a consulting activity there is usually a large amount of exchange of information and materials between the consultant and client. Access to the consultant in person, through the mail, or over the phone will be necessary throughout the length of the consulting contract. It is, however, not essential for the consultant to perform their functions in person. For instance, a firm which is performing some marketing research activities can complete their functions from data banks and surveying at their offices rather than at the health organization. I have found that personal relations between the consultant and the client to be very important. Therefore, to develop trust and confidence between the two parties it is important to have effective lines of communication.

ORIENTATION TO THE CONSULTING SERVICE

Consultants vary in their expertise, educational background, and professional experience. Typically, consultants have a single or a few specialties. For example, they may specialize in performing marketing research, raising funds, selecting media channels, developing marketing plans, creating advertising campaigns, or monitoring public relations activities. It is important for the health administrator/medical provider to research their needs and match them with the most effective service available. A good consultant will inform the client of his/her expertise and even refer the client to quality resources for other specialties. However, some firms have access internally or externally to key specialists in different marketing areas.

One firm may be able to meet all of your marketing needs or several firms may be hired to perform specialized functions.

SPECIFIC RECOMMENDATIONS IN MAKING THE EXPERIENCE OF USING MARKETING CONSULTANTS COST-EFFECTIVE

The following section outlines some key steps which can assist in the consulting experience being more productive.

1. Do some reading in general marketing before meeting with the consultant. In other words, read some basic marketing textbook so that you have a basic understanding of terminology and methodologies typically used in marketing. This will allow you to ask better questions and to understand the strategies being presented by the consultant. A good technique that I have personally found rewarding is to invite my clients to a seminar on marketing being given by myself or others. This can also be accomplished by holding an initial educational session with the providers and their staffs.

2. Think about what you want to achieve with marketing and ways you have considered marketing your services. This means that a specific list of goals and objectives outlining exactly what you want to achieve is essential. Also, make a list of ways in which you have already marketed the organization before meeting with the consultants. This will prevent duplication and provide the consultants with a strong guideline to follow in achieving your agreed upon marketing goals and objectives.

3. Make up a preliminary budget reflecting the amount of money your organization would be willing to spend on marketing activities. This will allow you to work within your means and be better able to evaluate the financial projections made by the consultant related to their expenses.

4. Make a list of questions you have about the consultant's services and procedures. Be ready to ask the consultant for specifics as to his/her methodology and work practices for marketing the organization.

5. Set up a preliminary meeting with a potential consultant to orient the principals of the firm. This meeting will allow you to evaluate your compatibility with the consultant, review the consultant's approach to marketing, obtain a client referral list from the consultant, and most importantly, request a formal proposal and budget estimate from the consultant.

6. If you hire the consultant, make sure a formal contract is written up and evaluated by your attorney. Do not let friendship prevent you from formalizing a contract.

7. Have the consultant make a thorough internal and external review of your existing organization or service in order to become better acquainted with your staff, facilities, markets.

8. If you have an established service, make sure the consultant performs an audit of your historical and current clients/patients in order to stimulate better targeting for future clients/patients.

9. Make sure you plan a regular meeting time and date for the consultant to keep you abreast of his/her activities and for you to continually inform the consultant about anything new in your service.

10. Do not keep information about your service a secret from your consultant in order for the services to be cost-effective. For example, a consultant was hired to develop a marketing plan for a local health organization. The consultant developed strategies based on a thorough marketing audit. After finishing the plan, the client indicated that another consultant had been hired a year earlier to perform some marketing research. This information should have been supplied so duplication and expense were prevented.

11. Make sure there is good communication between you and the consultant. It is a two-way relationship. You should expect to be kept informed and vice versa. I cannot emphasize this point enough, as miscommunication, or a lack of it, can be most damaging to the project's effectiveness and your relationship with the consultant.

12. An important criterion is to pay attention to the advice your consultant is giving you about marketing your service. Unfortunately, there is an old saying that "everybody knows something about marketing." I'm sure your staff members and even your patients will comment on what would be best in marketing your organization. Just as you are able to provide advice in your specialty, so does the marketer. This does not mean you should follow advice blindly. Ask questions just as the patient should related to a treatment plan prescribed for him. However, if you plan on reaping the rewards of marketing experience, relate to your consultant as a professional just as you expect others to respect you in your profession.

13. Try to be patient about getting results. Marketing takes time. It is also not a one-shot activity. A true marketing program requires long-term development. In fact, marketing will be part of your daily activities for as long as your organization exists. Therefore, do not

expect miracles overnight. Expect results to occur gradually. If results do occur faster than planned, you are that much more ahead of plan. A good marketer will not promise you immediate results, but a professional buildup of clients over time. Beware of the miracle "fixer-uppers."

14. Make sure the consultant educates you about his/her progress. You should become knowledgeable in many of the activities which the consultant implements so that you can better evaluate future marketing needs. This will also allow you not to become totally dependent upon the consultant. A quality consultant will adequately educate you about procedures so you can perform some of the marketing functions in the future by yourself, if you wish.

15. Understanding and believing in marketing is important. Marketing is not immoral, unethical, or illegal. It is also not just advertising or public relations. Give marketing a chance. Hiring a consultant when you may not understand or believe in the practice of marketing can be a waste of money. Work with your consultant to learn about the many benefits that marketing can offer.

16. Organize staff meetings so that the consultant can keep your staff informed of any progress. You may play this important role instead by staying in contact with the consultant and communicating the progress to your staff and board.

17. Remember that the consultant is not your enemy or a competitor. The consultant has a mutual benefit in seeing you succeed. Open up a communication line with them, listen to their advice, and be decisive when the consultant asks your advice or to make a decision. For example, a client asked me to develop a new brochure for them. I developed a final copy before printing it and reviewed it with them. I asked them to carefully examine it and decide whether they were satisfied. They okayed it and I printed thousands. One week later they changed their minds and wanted to re-write the brochure. In order to avoid wasting time, money, and energy make sure you take the time to think about a decision and stick to it.

18. Make sure you participate in all major decisions, i.e., a new brochure, an advertisement, a speech, or a mailing. You will have to live with your decisions for a long time. All of the marketing activities represent your services. Feel comfortable with the activities and discuss them with the consultant.

19. Be aware of considerable indirect costs that are involved in marketing. For example, if you were mailing the service's brochures to the local community, most expenses related to postage,

stuffing, and labeling would not be included in your typical consultant's fee. These expenses are added to your marketing financial outlays. Have the consultant give you a realistic estimate of the added expenses before an activity is implemented.

20. The consultant you negotiate with originally needs to be the one who will be accountable for your project. Many times large firms have partners negotiate a contract and then inexperienced staff actually do the work and take over the account. It is important when someone is marketing your services to be involved throughout the project for continuity.

21. Just as there are good and poor medical providers, it is no different with consultants. Marketing consultants vary in educational and professional experience and knowledge. Make sure you hire a consultant who is educationally trained in marketing health and human services and has a strong background in marketing your type of service.

22. Stick to your originally agreed upon plan. Do not panic if clients/patients are not knocking down your doors right after an open house or even a formal advertising plan. Most good marketers realize that long-term benefits will materialize if the plan is given half a chance.

23. Your marketing consultant requires access to other consultants you might have hired. For example, if you were opening a new wing of a clinic and you hired a construction contractor, an interior decorator, or even a general management consultant who is developing systems, the marketing consultant has to coordinate his/her activities with them. The facilities, decor, and even data systems, for example, are components of marketing.

24. A good consultant will be honest with their evaluation and strategies. They will not just say what you want to hear. For example, I had a client who just loved their interior decorating. I felt strongly that it was inappropriate for the type of patients they were serving. It would have been a disservice to my client if I agreed with her just because they were paying me. Honest communication between client and consultant can be irritating at times, but beneficial in the long run.

25. The marketing consultant should write a formal marketing plan for you before implementing any strategies. Do not approach marketing on a piecemeal basis. Marketing is a process. Multiple components need to be coordinated and included in any successful marketing endeavor. A formal plan can act as a guide which you and

the marketer can constantly monitor for future actions. The plan can also act as a control system in order to measure the effectiveness of your marketing endeavors.

26. Many marketing endeavors have failed due to the lack of support from medical staffs or boards. The marketer requires direct access to these groups to assist in marketing and to keep them informed. If this is not possible then a marketing subcommittee or the main administrator can act as an intermediate.

27. Before most marketing strategies such as advertising are implemented have them evaluated by legal counsel for any potential problems.

28. Give the consultant access to all key administrative and medical personnel and most records and data.

29. Frustration occurs when the consultant involved in developing a marketing plan is not part of implementation. If you establish confidence in the consultant attempt to have the same firm involved with implementing the marketing strategies.

30. It may also be valuable to have the consultant "on call" for advice even after the initial projects are completed. A long-term relationship may prove to be very effective.

The marketing consultant can be a major resource in marketing your organization. It is hoped that some of these suggestions will be helpful in nurturing a cost-effective relationship with the marketing consultant.

Appendix C:
Using Computers in Health Marketing

A key aspect of marketing in today's health environment is the collection of audit information about internal and external environments. Many times the collection, storage, assimilation, and retrieval of this information can be a time consuming aspect of health care marketing. Therefore, a computer system can provide assistance for the health marketer in deciding 1) what information is needed; 2) where it can be obtained; and 3) how it can be reported and analyzed. A marketing information system can be quite different from systems utilized in other business disciplines within the health organization. Most systems handle day-to-day operational transactions for such areas as payroll, medical records, admissions, etc. In comparison most marketing data systems apply to answering questions from a variety of perspectives: strategies, targeting, customers, competition, market, etc. The marketing information system can be the central point of interrelationships with other major departments in the health organization. These relationships are depicted by the following areas.

A marketing information system interacts with:

Administration
Finance
Personnel
Medical Records
Admissions
Patient Care
Planning
Research and Development
Nursing
Medical/Clinical Staff
Ambulatory Services
External Environment

The marketing information system revolves around the decision-making needs of the director of marketing. The following list describes the interrelationship of the types of information required for effective marketing. A marketing information system can provide:

1. Governmental statistical analysis
2. Customer profiles
3. Competitor analysis
4. Health industry reports
5. Segmentation and targeting reports
6. Control and evaluation analysis of marketing strategies
7. New service feasibility analysis
8. Media and placement analysis
9. Client survey results
10. Time lines for service and strategy implementation
11. Financial forecasts
12. Marketing mix decision analysis
13. Profitability analysis for each service

APPLICATIONS

There are many different types of applications for the computer in health care marketing. This section outlines several of these activities.

Market Data Report

An important aspect of being a health care marketer today is the need to stay ahead and keep abreast of market changes in health care. The market data requirements today are so broad that the health marketer must rely on marketing research firms, information brokers, government sources, and other published market information. The market structure includes information about the economic, demographic, political, technological, cultural, and informational aspects of the health care industry within our service areas. The marketer must identify the market structure and parameters which require measurement and data collection for future strategy development. For example, the results of a sound computer-generated marketing data system can supply the data:

1. To segment and profile specific market characteristics of the health service;
2. To identify changes in the service market;

3. To measure market potential by socio-demographic variables;
4. To measure market penetration by service;
5. To measure competitor position by service;
6. To identify select market perceptions, values, and lifestyle profiles for service development and strategy implementation;
7. To measure potential impact of legislative changes on utilization of a service;
8. To measure market share;
9. To measure price and income elasticity of demand for the services;
10. To measure the service performance by service type;
11. To calculate competitive activity by market and geographic region;
12. To aid in marketing research activities;
13. To forecast trends in the industry and community;
14. To measure specific market variables and their impact on profitability for the services; and
15. To perform cost-benefit analysis for selection of service mix and target prioritizing.

Competition Analysis Report

All health organizations have begun to understand that competition is a key characteristic of their marketplaces. This function is gradually becoming a common use for the computer in health marketing. By systematically reviewing competitive data for their potential impact on your organization, it allows for an improved planning process. For example, a typical competitor analysis can be organized in the following fashion:

COMPETITOR ANALYSIS REPORT

Competitive Data	Competitor	Your Service Data
Name		
Service Line		
Service Mix		
Service Characteristic		
Geographic Coverage		

Competitive Data	Competitor	Your Service Data
Current Utilization		
Service Utilization Capacity		
Share of Market		
Promotional Method		
Advertising Channels		
History (length of service)		
Quality and Performance Record		
Uniqueness in Market		
Market Positioning Statement		

Strategy Mix Report

Tracking the implementation and effectiveness of different marketing strategies can be a cost-effective tool of your computer. For example, just generating a report which monitors the promotional activities for the health organization can be useful. The following report is an example of a promotional monitoring device for the marketer:

PROMOTIONAL MIX ACTIVITY REPORT

Promotional Strategy	Date	Utilization Trend	Geographic Area Covered
Radio			
Television			
Press Releases			
Social Events			
Journal Advertisements			
Educational Programs			
Direct Mail Campaigns			
Newspaper Advertisements			
Sponsorship of Sport Events			

Market Segmentation Report

This report can be a very useful one as it outlines service segments. Market profile information is generated targeting and competitor analysis.

MARKET SEGMENTATION REPORT

Service	Targets for Your Organization	Targets Covered by Competitor A
Service X	Adults over 65 Incomes over $15,000 Living in eastern part of city	55-65 age group Incomes over $10,000 Living all over county
Service Y	Two-Income families Families with one child Single Parents	Male heads-of-household Families with more than two children
Service Z	Disabled Adults	Only disabled adults referred by court
	Minority Disabled Adults	Adults of minority and non-minority groups

ACCESS TO COMPUTER HARDWARE, SOFTWARE, AND DATA

These types of reports can be generated by all sizes of computers. Today, the microcomputer can be purchased for a marketing department with screens, multiple disk drives, adequate storage capabilities, and select software for well under $5,000. During the next few years these machines will be getting smaller, lighter, and even less expensive as competition expands. Before long there will be many microcomputers capable of fitting in a brief case with the ability to tie into an organization's main frame computer. Because of the flexibility and quality products coming into the market, it does not have to be a major investment when beginning to utilize the computer for the health marketing department.

An important decision is to select effective software for the computer. Many organizations now produce software packages for automatic input of data into predesigned report mechanisms. In other words, the marketer can actually generate a wide array of reports without having to program. These predeveloped software programs allow for forecasting, record keeping, filing, etc. An important point to remember is to have a professional assist in deciding on software applicability to your system and needs. Software packages can be purchased from a variety of vendors such as: computer firms, software dealers, trade associations, software directories, marketing research firms, and universities. There are several software reference texts available on the market to assist in selecting software for your needs. When buying software packages make sure the instruction documentation is clear and complete for your comprehension. If you are not sure about vendors of software packages, call around to several marketing research firms in your area. Most of these people can be very helpful in leading you to directories and individual companies. For example, one of the most complete directories on the market, titled *Softwhere,* is published by Moore Data Management Services in Minneapolis, Minnesota. This directory supplies the reader with a thorough source reference of software for the entire health care industry including program descriptions, current prices, warranty information, etc.

Another source of data is through time sharing systems which are geared toward planning processes. Timesharing vendors are listed in the yellow pages of most phone books and contract with your organization to provide up-to-date market information. Timesharing allows you to not have to keep massive data files yourself but to have sporadic access to records through a rental or leasing arrangement. Through an inexpensive modem, or telecommunications hookup with your microcomputer, you can network with the firm's main computer data base. This can also be very helpful if your health organization has multiple sites and data access is needed. Vendors do specialize in various functions such as forecasting, market analysis, risk analysis, demographic data bases, planning and financial modeling, and even graphics. For example, firms such as Control Data, General Electric, Tymshare, NCR, and McDonnell Douglas are timeshare vendors.

An alternative source of marketing information is a fee-for-service data vendor. In other words, there are marketing research firms which can tailor your marketing needs with appropriate data bases and you pay for these select services. For example, one firm, CACI, Inc. in Arlington, Virginia, converts Census Bureau computer tapes into some 30 types of reports. You can call a toll free number and have your report mailed within 24 hours. One of the most useful of these reports is the demographic report which shows population, number of households, average family size, racial distribution, age distribution, per capita income, average family income, and average household income for a select geographic region. You can choose your own market size by supplying the street intersection representing your center of interest and receiving an analysis covering a radius from a few blocks to several miles. The costs usually run from around $100 for the first report and a lower fee for additional reports each time you change the radius. Before entering into the purchasing of this kind of information, it is important to outline your exact data needs, find out if this information is available from these vendors, shop around for price quotations, ask about the format in which the information will be provided, and determine the frequency in which you might need this information. The American Marketing Association and their local chapters can be very helpful in identifying lists of these types of research data firms.

Graphic presentations can be a very useful tool for marketers, especially when formal presentations to administration and boards are involved. Graphs, plots, and charts can be generated by microcomputer systems. Computer graphics printers, plotters, and software packages are relatively inexpensive and can be adaptable to almost any type of computer. Graphics packages provide information through 1) time series graphs with a point-by-point record of a trend over time (forecasting by service and geographic location); 2) scatter plot presentations offering a comparison of two sets' of data (comparison of one service's utilization to another); 3) bar charts (profit and loss by service item, utilization by service); 4) histograms (number of questionnaire responses by day or week); and 5) pie charts (market segments, utilization by geographic region). However, the most modern packages can now allow for pictures to be drawn in multiple colors, shading, overlays, and various configurations. Microcomputer graphics provide the health marketer with an invaluable tool at a very reasonable price. It is recommended that the marketer request the software vendor for a demonstration on your type of computer and printer before purchasing the package. Matching your presentation needs and the quality and capability of the package's output is essential.

This brief scenario is intended to stimulate the health marketer to experiment with various ways to improve productivity. The computer and professionally prepared data can improve the marketing function and prove cost-effective if done properly. One word of caution is that most health marketers have not yet begun to utilize computers in their planning process. Therefore, it is important to shop around; research the different sources of computers, software, and research firms; and not go overboard in purchasing data resources which are beyond the needs of the organization or the capabilities of the staff.

Appendix D:
Working with the Media

One of the recent changes for health administrators has been the need to interact with the media. In fact, media relations have become one of the most important facets of marketing a health care organization. It is also the area in which most administrators are inexperienced. Therefore, this short appendix provides a survey of key points to developing a successful media program. These key points include:

1. *Organizational Media Policy:* Before any administrator has contact with the media it is wise to develop an organizational policy toward the media. In other words, a formal policy document should be drawn up for the release of information. This document should include the organization's philosophy toward the media, a survey of the exact kinds and amounts of information which will be released to the media, and the identification of the people who are authorized to release information to the media.

2. *Media Release Format:* Media information needs to conform to standards related to content, style, placement, and timing. The content can be formulated to fit a set amount of information and written in a style which is sensitive to the media channel being utilized. Placement relates to the type of media which is selected. For example, media channels include newspapers, television stations, radio stations, wire services, journals, newsletters, bulletins, etc. Each of these media channels require unique types and formats of information. TV, for example, is very interested in visual aids and radio requires catchy script. When developing outlines for different formats the people associated with each of these media channels can be very helpful in terms of giving advice as to the release formats they desire.

3. *Developing Relationship with Key Media Personnel:* One of the most important aspects of making media relationships successful is the necessity to get to know key media professionals. For example, these people can include local newspaper editors, radio and TV news editors, or the local health reporters.

4. *Provide Leads to Other Stories Besides Your Own:* A good way to receive fair treatment by the media is to share leads on topical stories which may, or may not, be related to your own health organization. For example, having lunch with the local health editor of the newspaper and just discussing current trends in the industry and key events going on can lead the editor to new story lines. Many times in return that editor may be favorable to a story about your organization periodically in the future.

5. *Make Your Message Interesting:* The news market is oversaturated. Therefore, a unique position has to be identified. For example, unique positions include "being the first of its kind," having celebrities endorse the service, or indicating that the service "fulfills a real health need of the community." The event must catch the interest of the reader or listener without being overdramatic or sensationalized.

6. *Most News Space Is Routine:* Besides the unique position, it is important to remember that most newspapers, for example, report just average local news about events. Therefore, developing quality news releases about everyday events or services can prove effective.

7. *Establish Credibility Through News Releases:* The news release can be very important for communicating with the press and broadcast media. However, releases should be developed selectively to prove your credibility and reliability as a news source. Just churning them out on a monthly basis, for example, may actually damage this important credibility. Journalists are overwhelmed with news releases and this type of credible selectivity may prove to be more cost-effective.

8. *Key Access to Local Newspapers:* Sometimes we tend to not take local newspapers seriously in relation to national ones. However, there is no greater access to a local market than through the local paper. Local newspapers are concerned mainly with communicating information about issues and services in the local community.

9. *Don't Overlook Other Local Print Media:* For example, media channels in the local community may include weekly newspapers, religious or social group newspapers, community magazines or newsletters, free advertiser-supported "shoppers," community bulletin boards, union bulletins, school district flyers and newsletters, chamber of commerce directories, local college newspapers, letters to the editor, local advice columns, and community calendars. No matter how small the print media it cannot be overlooked.

10. *Use Local Radio Effectively:* TV and radio accounts for the

majority of information about current events. Radio can be very cost-effective as it usually is less expensive than TV and is targeted at specific audiences according to the individual station. Radio is also listened to in a variety of settings and activities—while working, driving, eating, etc. It is also possible to target to all-news stations as in cable news on TV. There is an opportunity to get public service announcements mentioned on radio more easily than on TV. These PSAs can be read during newscasts, editorials, or public affairs programs. The key contact people at radio stations are program directors or public service coordinators. They can also be very helpful in even organizing formal interviews which can be integrated into main news stories or allowing for key personnel from the health organization to be guests on panel or call-in shows.

11. *The Most Influential Media—Television:* We have reached the point in time when a whole generation has been nurtured by TV. Many of our interests and values have been influenced by this media channel. It has become the channel with the greatest impact in terms of the size and diversity of the audience. It is important to remember that TV includes VHF, UHF, and CATV systems. VHF stations have the strongest signals and usually include national networks such as NBC, CBS, and ABC. These stations usually have the largest audiences. UHF stations have smaller audiences but access to them is easier than the VHF ones. CATV, or cable stations, are gradually becoming some of the most important ones for more selective targeting. Contacting personnel at stations can vary as to their source. For example, such staff members as public affairs coordinators, news directors, reporters, producers, and directors can provide access. One interesting note—the station manager is usually not involved with program planning. There are also many different forms of information which can be provided: public service announcements, local news stories, news releases, formal written stories, free speeches, editorial responses, community service announcements, talk show interviews, call-in program guest spots, or even special shows on select topics of need in the community. Most stations are constantly seeking new story lines since variety is a key ingredient to a successful station.

12. *Developing the Network:* There is nothing more important than constantly reinforcing media contacts. The networking process is vital to a successful media campaign. Too many marketers and directors of public relations tend to neglect this area of marketing. Networking with key personnel in all media channels can prove very

beneficial for the long-run survival and prosperity of the organization. One of the first steps for developing a network is to survey the wide range of media resources that are available in the community. The second step is to survey additional resources of information about the media from local Chamber of Commerce, United Way, Urban League, Family Service Agency of America, and other agencies which may have directories of local media channels. Local college libraries may possess media directories as well as classes in communication and media presentation skills. Once these media channels are identified, contact the key personnel through phone calls, appointments, or by letter. Most media professionals are very cooperative. In this contact, the individual needs of the media channel must become known. For example, each channel is unique in answering 1) who you contact; 2) what types and formats of information they are seeking; 3) why they should be interested in your news item; 4) where the information should be channeled; and 5) when the information should be submitted. It is important to meet deadlines as most media personnel are under extreme pressure to meet their own deadlines. The relationship between the health organization and the media professional must be mutually beneficial. Your organization will benefit from the publicity and the media professional will fill a news gap in their programming.

13. *Basic Questions to Answer:* As a final point, the health organization requires some planning before entering a relationship with the media. In other words, you must answer the following:

a) *What message do you want to communicate?*—i.e., inform about a health problem, publicize a select service, etc.
b) *Who should receive this message?*—i.e., general community, parents, etc.
c) *Which media channel is most effective?*—i.e., newspaper, radio, TV, etc.
d) *What form of media presentation is most important?*—i.e., article, news release, letter to the editor, interview, public service announcement, editorial, etc.

Additional Literary References
in Health Marketing

1. *Marketing Health and Human Services* by Rubright, Aspen, 1982.
2. *Marketing Your Hospital* by MacMillan, AHA, 1981.
3. *Marketing Planning and Strategies* by Jain, South-Western, 1981.
4. *Strategic Planning in Health Care* by Flexner, Aspen, 1981.
5. *Strategic Market Planning* by Abell, Prentice-Hall, 1981.
6. *Marketing for Non-Profit Organizations* by Radia, Auburn House, 1979.
7. *Marketing the Service Sector* by Rathnell, Wentrop, 1980.
8. *Marketing Health Care* by MacStravic, Aspen, 1980.
9. *Marketing by Objectives for Hospitals* by MacStravic, Aspen, 1981.
10. *Issues in Health Care Marketing* by Cooper, Aspen, 1981.
11. *Strategic Planning in Health Services Management* by Fournet, Aspen, 1982.
12. *Health Care Marketing Management—A Case Approach* by Cooper, Aspen, 1982.
13. *Marketing for Non-Profit Organizations* by Kotler, Prentice-Hall, 1982.
14. *Strategic Marketing Plan Master Guide* by Stevens, Prentice-Hall, 1982.
15. *Marketing Health Services* by Cooper, Aspen, 1983.
16. *The Marketing Imagination* by Levitt, Free Press, 1984.
17. *Services Marketing* by Lovelock, Prentice-Hall, 1984.
18. *Marketing Professional Services* by Kotler, Prentice-Hall, 1984.
19. *The Mind of the Strategist* by Ohmae, Penguin Books, 1982.
20. *Health Care Marketing Plans: From Strategy to Action* by Hillestad and Berkowitz, Dow Jones-Irwin, 1984.
21. *Strategic Advertising Campaigns* by Schultz, Martin and Brown, 2nd edition, 1984.
22. *Life-Styled Marketing* by Hanan, American Management Association, 1980.
23. *Financial Dimensions of Marketing Management* by Mossman, Wiley, 1978.

24. *Marketing for Public and NonProfit Managers* by Lovelock and Weinberg, Wiley, 1984.

25. *The Mirror Makers* by Fox, Morrow Books, 1984.

26. *Ogilvy On Advertising* by David Ogilvy, Crown Books, 1984.

27. *Marketing Professional Services* by Kotler, Prentice-Hall, 1984.

28. *Bibliography on Health Care Marketing, 1979-83* edited by Philip Cooper, American Marketing Association, 1985.

Journals

1. *Health Care Planning and Marketing* by MacStravic, Aspen (Quarterly), 1981 (discontinued).

2. *Journal of Health Care Marketing* by B. J. Dunlap, Appalachian State University, Quarterly, 1981 to present.

3. *Journal of Marketing* by American Marketing Association, quarterly, 1952 to present.

4. *Profiles in Hospital Marketing* by Wentworth Publishing, quarterly.

5. *Target Marketing* by American Marketing Association, monthly.

6. *Health Marketing Quarterly,* edited by Wm. J. Winston, Haworth Press, New York; first issue Fall, 1983.

7. *Journal of Professional Services Marketing,* edited by Wm. J. Winston, Haworth Press, New York; first issue Fall, 1985.

8. *Psychotherapy Marketing and Practice Development Reports,* edited by Wm. J. Winston and Rosanna Pribilovics, Haworth Press, New York; first issue Spring, 1985.

Associations

ACADEMY OF HEALTH CARE MARKETING, American Marketing Association, Chicago, 1980 to present.
AMERICAN COLLEGE OF HEALTH CARE MARKETING, Washington, D.C., 1984 to present.